Taxcafe.co.uk Tax Guides

Non-Resident & Offshore Tax Planning

By Lee Hadnum LLB ACA CTA

Important Legal Notices:

Taxcafe®
TAX GUIDE - "Non-Resident and Offshore Tax Planning"

Published by:
Taxcafe UK Limited
67 Milton Road
Kirkcaldy KY1 1TL
Tel: (0044) 01592 560081
Email: team@taxcafe.co.uk

13th Edition, April 2012

ISBN 978-1-907302-56-5

Disclaimer
Before reading or relying on the content of this tax guide please read the disclaimer carefully.

Other Taxcafe guides by the same author

Using a Company to Save Tax

Tax Saving Tactics for Non-Doms

The World's Best Tax Havens

Selling Your Business

Disclaimer

1. Please note that this publication is intended as **general guidance only** and does NOT constitute accountancy, tax, financial or other professional advice. The author and Taxcafe UK Limited make no representations or warranties with respect to the accuracy or completeness of the contents of this publication and cannot accept any responsibility for any liability, loss or risk, personal or otherwise, which may arise, directly or indirectly, from reliance on information contained in this publication.

2. Please note that tax legislation, the law and practices of government and regulatory authorities (e.g. Revenue & Customs) are constantly changing. Furthermore, your personal circumstances may vary from the general information contained in this tax guide which may not be suitable for your situation. We therefore recommend that for accountancy, tax, financial or other professional advice, you consult a suitably qualified accountant, tax specialist, independent financial adviser, or other professional adviser. Your professional adviser will be able to provide specific advice based on your personal circumstances.

3. Please note that Taxcafe UK Limited has relied wholly on the expertise of the author in the preparation of the content of this publication. The author is not an employee of Taxcafe UK Limited but has been selected by Taxcafe UK Limited using reasonable care and skill to write the content of this publication.

4. All persons described in the examples in this guide are entirely fictional characters created specifically for the purposes of this guide. Any similarities to actual persons, living or dead, or to fictional characters created by any other author, are entirely coincidental.

About the Author

Lee is a rarity among tax advisers having both legal and chartered accountancy qualifications. After qualifying as a prize winner in the Institute of Chartered Accountants entrance exams, he went on to become a Chartered Tax Adviser (CTA).

Having worked in Ernst & Young's tax department for a number of years, Lee decided to start his own tax consulting firm, specialising in capital gains tax, inheritance tax and business tax planning.

Whenever he has spare time he enjoys DIY, walking and travelling.

Contents

1. Introduction   **1**

2. Residence, Ordinary Residence & Domicile   **4**

2.1   Why do Residence & Domicile Matter?   4
2.2   Becoming Non-Resident   5
2.3   Recent Court of Appeal Decisions   9
2.4   Days Spent in the UK   15
2.5   Statutory Residence Test   16
2.6   The Importance of 'Ordinary Residence'   23
2.7   Ordinary Residence When Coming to the UK   24
2.8   Residence in a Nutshell   29
2.9   Why Domicile Is So Important   31
2.10 Watch Out for this Inheritance Tax Trap   33

3. How to Become Non-Resident   **34**

3.1   What You Stand to Gain   34
3.2   Convincing the Taxman You Are Non-Resident   35
3.3   How to Avoid Timing Traps   43
3.4   How the Taxman Decides Residence Status   44
3.5   Offshore Checklist   45

4. How to Avoid UK Income Tax   **49**

4.1   Introduction   49
4.2   Rental Income   50
4.3   Interest & Royalties   50
4.4   Dividends   51
4.5   Pension Income   53
4.6   Personal Allowance   54
4.7   Making Pension Contributions   56
4.8   Employment Income   56
4.9   UK National Insurance   59
4.10 Pension Planning   62
4.11 Out of the Frying Pan and into the Fire   66
4.12 UK Company Owners Moving Overseas   67

5. How to Avoid UK Capital Gains Tax   **69**

5.1 Introduction   69

5.2 Countries with Generous CGT Rules   69

5.3 Exceptions to the Five Year Rule   72

5.4 Traps to Avoid in the Year You Depart   73

5.5 Out of the Frying Pan and into the Fire   73

5.6 Postponing Disposals and Avoiding CGT   75

5.7 Avoiding CGT on Business Assets   76

5.8 Sale of a Former Home   77

5.9 Favourable Tax Jurisdictions   78

5.10 Using Enterprise Investment Schemes   80

5.11 Offshore Investments for UK Residents   81

5.12 Making the Most of Tax-free Capital Gains   83

5.13 Sell Property Before or After Returning to the UK?   85

6. How to Avoid Inheritance Tax   **89**

6.1 Introduction   89

6.2 How to Lose Your UK Domicile   89

6.3 How Domicile Status is Determined   91

6.4 How to Establish an Overseas Domicile   93

6.5 Retaining Your Domicile of Origin   94

6.6 Moving Abroad to Lose UK Deemed Domicile   95

7. The Advantages of Being Non-Domiciled   **98**

7.1 Non-UK Domiciliaries   98

7.2 The Remittance Tax Charge Explained   99

7.3 Planning for the £30,000 Tax Charge   107

7.4 Planning for the £50,000 Tax Charge   109

7.5 Capital & Income Accounts   110

7.6 Married Couples   112

7.7 Residence   113

7.8 Income-Free Investments   113

7.9 The New Remittance Tax Rules - FAQs   114

7.10 Gifting Assets Abroad to Avoid Remittance Rules   118

7.11 How the Remittance Basis Applies to Overseas Gains   120

7.12 Buying Property Overseas   121

7.13 Effect of UK Domicile Status on UK Inheritance Tax   124

8. Working Overseas: A Powerful Tax Shelter   127
8.1 Introduction   127
8.2 Tax-Deductible Expenses   128
8.3 Tax-Free Termination Payments   129
8.4 Protecting Your Property Investments
        from the Taxman   130

9. Making Use of Double Tax Relief   133
9.1 Introduction   133
9.2 Credit Relief   133
9.3 Expense Relief   134

10. Tax Benefits of Offshore Trusts   136
10.1 Introduction   136
10.2 How Offshore Trusts Are Taxed   136
10.3 Capital Gains Tax Consequences   137
10.4 Inheritance Tax Consequences   138
10.5 Dangers for UK Domiciliaries   139
10.6 When an Offshore Trust Can Save You Tax   140
10.7 UK Resident but Not UK Domiciled   143
10.8 Tax Treatment of Distributions from Offshore
         Trusts to UK Residents   146
10.9   UK Protectors and Offshore Trusts   149
10.10 Where Do You Set Up a Trust and
          How Much Does It Cost?   150
10.11 Using Trusts for Asset Protection   152
10.12 Keeping a Low Profile   158

11. Tax Benefits of Offshore Companies   161
11.1 Introduction   161
11.2 How the Taxman Spots Phony
         Offshore Management   162
11.3 Role of Managing Director   163
11.4 Recent Case on Company Residence   163
11.5 Apportionment of Capital Gains   167
11.6 Benefits in Kind   168
11.7 Using a Non-Resident Trust and Company   168

11.8 Using an Offshore Company and Trust:
      Non-UK Domiciliaries   170
11.9 How to Use Your Spouse's Offshore Status   171
11.10 Personal Service Companies   177
11.11 Transfer Pricing Rules   178
11.12 Types of Offshore Entity   179
11.13 Overseas Trading   186
11.14 UK Controlled Foreign Company (CFC) Rules   188
11.15 UK Corporation Tax Planning After You've
      Left the UK   192

12. Investing in UK Property: A Case Study   196
12.1 Direct Ownership   196
12.2 Using a Trust to Own the Property   198
12.3 Using an Offshore Company   199
12.4 Tax Planning for Non-Residents Owning UK
      Property Investment Companies   199
12.5 Conclusion   202

13. Becoming a Tax Nomad   203

14. Double Tax Treaties   205
14.1 How Double Tax Treaties Work   205
14.2 What a Typical DTT Looks Like   205
14.3 The UK-Isle of Man Double Tax Treaty   209
14.4 Using Double Tax Treaties to Save Tax   211
14.5 Treaty Relief   212
14.6 Living or Buying Property in Spain   213
14.7 Capital Gains Tax in Other Countries   219
14.8 Countries without a UK Double Tax Treaty   221
14.9 How an Estate Tax Treaty Can Be Used   223

15. Buying Property Abroad   226
15.1 Introduction   226
15.2 UK Resident/Ordinarily Resident and Domiciled   226
15.3 Non-Resident/Ordinarily Resident and
      Non-UK Domiciled   227

15.4 UK Resident/Ordinarily Resident and
      Non-UK Domiciled   227
15.5 Use of an Offshore Company/Trust   230
15.6 Using Mixed Residence Partnerships to Avoid CGT   231
15.7 What About Overseas Tax Implications?   232
15.8 Double Tax Relief (DTR)   233
15.9 Summary   234

Appendix I: UK-Spain Double Tax Treaty   236

Appendix II: UK Treatment of Overseas Entities   237

Chapter 1

Introduction

This guide is designed to help those living or working abroad pay less tax on their UK income and investments. It also contains important information for those who live in the UK but wish to use the offshore tax rules to shelter their income and gains from the taxman.

This is an important and sophisticated area of tax planning. Moving yourself or your assets abroad is in many respects the ultimate form of tax avoidance and in some cases it is possible to reduce your tax bill to zero. However, there are also many traps to avoid and pitfalls to negotiate.

This publication highlights some of the key tax-planning opportunities and dangers, focusing on the UK's four major taxes: income tax, capital gains tax, inheritance tax and corporation tax.

Throughout we have tried to keep tax jargon to a minimum and illustrate the main points with examples.

A significant portion of the guide is devoted to the potential non-resident – individuals who are considering moving overseas and have heard that this may bring with it substantial tax benefits.

We look at the tax-saving opportunities, as well as the practical steps and dangers to bear in mind, when considering a move abroad.

In Chapter 2 we explain the concept of 'non residence' which has a huge effect on the amount of income tax and capital gains tax you pay. Details are provided of the proposed new statutory residence test that will be introduced in 2013. We also explain the concept of 'domicile', as there are a number of special rules for individuals who are UK resident but not UK domiciled. Domicile is also crucial when it comes to inheritance tax planning.

In Chapter 3 we list the steps you need to take to convince the taxman that you are non-resident and discuss some of the traps the authorities have set to catch 'phoney emigrants'.

Chapters 4, 5 and 6 take a detailed look at income tax, capital gains tax and inheritance tax-planning strategies for non-residents. The information contained in these chapters is extremely important for any would-be tax exile or emigrant and should be read carefully.

In Chapter 7 we focus our attention on non-domiciled people living and working in the UK and explain how they can use their special status to obtain tax savings. There have been a lot of changes in this area in recent years. We look in detail at how these changes affect the tax position of non-domiciliaries living in the UK.

In Chapter 8 we look at the income tax, capital gains tax and inheritance tax implications of working and travelling overseas because, aside from the 'permanent emigrant', many reading this guide may be considering working abroad at some point. After reading this guide you should have a clear understanding of how working abroad will affect your UK tax position.

Chapter 9 explains how you can use a number of reliefs to avoid being taxed twice – once in the UK and again in another country.

Offshore trusts and offshore companies are sometimes viewed as the preserve of the very wealthy. This is not necessarily the case and we have outlined in Chapters 10 and 11 how these structures can help you save tax and how to avoid the detailed tax anti-avoidance rules.

Reducing tax on property investments is a top priority for many UK residents and non-residents. The guide contains numerous examples with a 'property theme' and in Chapter 12 we take a closer look at how non-resident and non-domiciled investors should structure their property purchases.

Your residence status is often the critical factor when it comes to paying both UK and foreign taxes. But what if you can avoid being resident in ANY country? In Chapter 13 we take a brief look at how you can become a 'tax nomad' and avoid both UK and overseas taxes.

Throughout this guide we attempt to identify practical steps that can be taken to mitigate UK tax, although the tax regime of any relevant overseas country should also be borne in mind.

This is where double tax treaties come in. In Chapter 14 we explain the importance of these treaties in further detail.

Finally, Chapter 15 takes an in-depth look at buying property abroad and how to plan your affairs to avoid both UK and overseas income tax and capital gains tax.

We occasionally use some abbreviations. In particular, capital gains tax may be referred to as CGT, inheritance tax as IHT and HM Revenue and Customs as HMRC.

A lot of expat and offshore tax planning depends on getting dates and timing right, so many of the examples are based on specific tax years.

Remember that the UK tax year runs from April 6th to April 5th.

The tax year running from April 6th 2012 to April 5th 2013 may be referred to as the 2012/2013 tax year or just 2012/13.

Finally, remember that offshore tax planning is an extremely complex area and the relevant tax legislation, as well as HMRC's practices, can change quickly. You should never take any action until you have spoken to a suitably qualified professional who can advise you based on your personal circumstances.

Chapter 2

Residence, Ordinary Residence & Domicile

2.1 WHY DO RESIDENCE & DOMICILE MATTER?

The short answer is, they affect the amount of tax you have to pay.

UK residents who are also UK domiciled (we'll explain domicile later) have to pay UK income tax and capital gains tax on their 'worldwide income and gains'. In other words, no matter where in the world your assets are located or in what country your income is earned, it all falls into the UK tax net.

Those who are UK resident but non-UK domiciled can choose to be exempt from UK income tax and capital gains tax on foreign income and gains, until such time as the money is remitted to the UK. As we shall see, however, choosing to be taxed under the remittance basis can be extremely expensive.

If you are a non-resident you do not have to pay UK tax on non-UK income. However, you still have to pay UK tax on your UK salary, business profits (if the business is carried out in the UK), pension income and investment income. There are, however, some special rules that can reduce the tax non-residents pay on some types of UK income.

Capital gains tax depends on both your residence and 'ordinary residence'. If you cease to be resident in the UK without also ceasing to be ordinarily resident here, you will remain liable to UK capital gains tax in respect of gains on your worldwide assets.

If an individual ceases to be both resident and ordinarily resident, he is outside the scope of UK capital gains tax, even on UK assets.

So clearly your residence and domicile have a huge effect on the size of your UK tax bill. The crucial question is how do you qualify for these reliefs and exemptions?

2.2   BECOMING NON-RESIDENT

HMRC's practice – based on a mixture of statute and court decisions – has historically been to regard you as resident in the UK during a tax year if:

- You spend 183 days or more in the UK during the tax year, or

- Although here for less than 183 days, you have spent more than 90 days per year in the country over the past three years (taken as an average). You will then be classed as UK resident from the fourth year.

For example, an individual who regularly returns to the UK for 87 days per tax year may still be regarded as UK resident.

Although the 90-day time limit is undoubtedly important, it is not necessarily decisive any longer. In various court cases in the last few years HMRC has argued that an emigrant remains UK resident if strong ties to the UK are retained.

This is a crucial point to remember.

Simply restricting your visits to the UK after you have left will not necessarily be enough to establish non UK residence.

The first change to this effect was in 2005 and came out of the Commissioners' decision in the 'Shepherd case'.

This case examined whether an airline pilot had ceased to be UK resident.

Mr Shepherd was an airline pilot employed by a British company, flying long-haul flights which started and ended at Heathrow. He retired on 22nd April 2000 and decided to live abroad. In October 1998 he started renting a flat in Cyprus and lived there before purchasing an apartment in 2002.

While working, he continued to stay in his UK family home before and after each flight, remained on the UK electoral roll and had all his correspondence sent to the UK.

The taxman said that he was UK resident as he remained in the UK for a settled purpose, to perform the duties of his employment and to continue to see his wife, family and friends.

Mr Shepherd argued that he had ceased to be resident, having established a new home in Cyprus.

His visits to the UK were less than 90 days, and the rest of his time was spent in Cyprus and flying (the majority of his time was actually spent flying).

The Special Commissioner found that his presence in the UK was substantial and continuous and there was no distinct break. Therefore he remained UK resident.

The crux of this decision was that Mr Shepherd worked in the UK, stayed in the family home and visited friends. In this context the simple fact that he had spent less than 90 days per tax year in the UK did not make him non UK resident.

In my view this decision was not surprising and essentially represents a change in emphasis, rather than a new change in practice.

The 90-day limit was never in itself a rule that established non UK residence. To actually establish non residence you would need to show that you have left the UK permanently (for at least three years) or for a settled purpose/employment, and that any UK visits averaged less than 90 days.

In this case, Mr Shepherd couldn't establish that his new life was overseas.

Therefore the impact of this case shouldn't be as widespread as the newspapers reported. Mr Shepherd's position was also made worse by the fact that he couldn't even establish 'treaty residence' in Cyprus (treaty residence is where a person is considered to be a resident in accordance with the terms of a tax treaty).

Another case ('Gaines-Cooper') looked at the method of calculating the 90 day average and could have important repercussions for those just under the limit.

As mentioned previously, it's never advisable to be in this predicament as the 90 day limit is not set in stone – if you approach this figure the taxman could argue that you are UK resident, especially where there is evidence showing you have strong UK ties. This was confirmed in the revised Revenue guidance issued in March 2009 which makes it clear that having close ties to the UK can still make you UK resident. In particular they have stated that:

"Your status is determined by the facts of your particular case. It is not simply a question of the number of days you spend in the country".

Previously Revenue and Customs accepted that, when calculating the number of days spent in the UK, the days of arrival and departure could be ignored. A common practice was to arrive on a Friday and depart on a Sunday. This would then be classed as only one day in the UK.

The Commissioners disagreed and argued that the number of nights spent in the UK should be considered. In the above example this would mean two days in the UK.

Revenue and Customs published guidance shortly after this stating there had been no change in their application of the 90 day rule.

However, as from 6th April 2008 new legislation has been introduced so that any day when you are present in the UK at midnight will be classed as a day spent in the UK for the purposes of the 183-day test. This will also usually apply to the 90-day test.

The key point is that you have to establish residence overseas. Only then does the 90 day rule come into the picture. If you then meet the 90 day rule you'll remain non-UK resident. If, however, you've never really left the UK you remain UK resident, whether or not you pass the 90-day test.

The Gaines-Cooper case looked at much more than just number of days spent in the UK when deciding a taxpayer's residence. The Commissioners decided to apply the law rather than the Revenue guidance. As we know, the law is pretty vague in this area so the

Commissioners said that residence should be given its natural and ordinary meaning.

As there is no legislation which lays down the required number of days spent in the UK, it's necessary to take into account all the facts of the case and look at a taxpayer's life in some detail.

The Commissioners stated that it's important to look at the existence of other ties to the UK, including the duration of an individual's presence in the UK, the number and frequency of visits, the place of birth, family and business ties and the nature of visits and other connections with the UK.

The availability of living accommodation in the UK should also be taken into account, although this has always been the case and traditional advice has been to sell or rent out any UK property prior to going overseas.

Most of these guidelines are common sense. The taxman wants to stop people claiming non residence solely on the grounds of days spent in the country, even though the UK is their home in all other respects.

In the Gaines-Cooper case, the Commissioners decided that the evidence added up to UK residence being retained: the individual was born in the UK, went to school here, had strong UK business ties, made regular visits, and his wife and son lived in the country.

As stated above, Revenue and Customs published a statement in January 2007 explaining that there has been no change in practice in relation to residence and the '91-day test'.

In particular, it states that the taxman will continue to:

- Follow the published guidance on residence and apply it fairly and consistently.
- Treat individuals who have not left the UK as remaining resident here.
- Consider all the relevant evidence, including the pattern of presence in the UK and elsewhere, to determine whether or not a person has left the UK.

This was also confirmed in the revised guidance that HMRC issued for non UK residents.

2.3   RECENT COURT OF APPEAL DECISIONS

A couple of decisions on UK residence have come out of the Court of Appeal during 2009 and 2010. These make very interesting reading for anyone thinking of becoming non-resident.

Grace Decision

This case also concerned an airline pilot. The individual worked for British Airways (BA), flying long-haul flights out of Gatwick and Heathrow. He had to be in England for several days before any outward flight and, in practice, sometimes between inward and outward flights.

From 1986 to 1997 he was resident in the UK but in August 1997 he took a rented apartment in Cape Town and then bought a house there. He argued that he became non UK resident at that point.

He regarded his house in Cape Town as his home and spent as much time there as he could. He also planned to retire there in the future.

HMRC argued that his continued presence in the UK, as the base from which he did his work, showed that he was still resident in the UK, just as he was before 1997.

The first thing the Court of Appeal did was agree with the High Court judge's list of factors that should be taken into account when determining residence:

"(i) The word "reside" is a familiar English word which means "to dwell permanently or for a considerable time, to have one's settled or usual abode, to live in or at a particular place". This is the definition taken from the Oxford English Dictionary in 1928 and is still the definition in the current on-line edition;

(ii) Physical presence in a particular place does not necessarily amount to residence in that place where, for example, a person's physical presence there is no more than a stop gap measure;

iii) In considering whether a person's presence in a particular place amounts to residence there, one must consider the amount of time that he spends in that place, the nature of his presence there and his connection with that place;

(iv) Residence in a place connotes some degree of permanence, some degree of continuity or some expectation of continuity;

(v) However, short but regular periods of physical presence may amount to residence, especially if they stem from performance of a continuous obligation (such as business obligations) and the sequence of visits excludes the elements of chance and of occasion;

(vi) Although a person can have only one domicile at a time, he may simultaneously reside in more than one place, or in more than one country;

(vii) Where a person has had his sole residence in the United Kingdom he is unlikely to be held to have ceased to reside in the United Kingdom (or to have "left" the United Kingdom) unless there has been a definite break in his pattern of life."

Crucially, this list confirms that, although some degree of permanence is required to establish residence, regular visits to the UK can amount to residence if they arise from an ongoing obligation (such as work commitments).

Distinct Break with the UK

The Court of Appeal also agreed with the High Court judge and reiterated the importance of making a distinct break with the UK.

The court stated that, in this case, there had not been a distinct break by the pilot:

"...The demands of his employment did not change in 1997, and the time which he spent in the UK attributable to his employment did not change. In that respect there was continuity in his pattern of existence. What did change was the place where he spent that part of his time when his whereabouts was not dictated by his employment..."

This is essentially as far as the Court of Appeal went:

"...I agree that a finding of residence is a possible conclusion, and perhaps a likely one, but it does not seem to me that it would be right for

the court to pre-empt the decision of the Special Commissioner on that issue..."

Although the Court of Appeal agreed with much of the High Court reasoning, the judges didn't go as far as to state that the pilot was UK resident. In their view this was a decision of fact and needed to be considered by the Special Commissioners (now the First Tier Tribunal).

They did however expressly state that, simply because he was in the UK on a regular basis because of his employment, this would not necessarily make him UK resident:

"...It seems to me that it would be wrong to treat the appellant's presence for the purposes of his employment as a factor which necessarily shows residence.

It may well be a strong pointer in that direction, but the decisions in Scotland, in the House of Lords and by Rowlatt J show clearly the need to take into account, weigh up and balance all relevant factors. I do not think it would be right to regard Mr Grace's presence in this country in order to perform the duties of his employment as a trump card which of itself concludes the issue in favour of residence..."

2011 Grace Decision

In February 2011 the case was passed back to the First Tier Tribunal which published its final judgement and found that Mr Grace was UK resident.

HMRC argued that residence has an 'adhesive' nature – it is harder for a person who has been resident to shake off resident status than it is for a person who has not been resident to show they have not acquired residence.

This is similar to the test for domicile and shows a definite convergence of HMRC's tests for losing residence and domicile.

The tribunal judge found that Mr Grace would need to show a sufficient break in the pattern of his life to convert his residency status to non residence (i.e., the 'distinct break' test that we looked at above).

The tribunal held that Mr Grace was resident in both the UK and South Africa. Mr Grace considered himself resident in South Africa only. He spent roughly equal amounts of time in both jurisdictions.

When he was in the UK, Mr Grace stayed at his house in Horley, where he had a settled abode. His presence in the UK was indefinite since that was where his employment was – and employment was a matter of choice.

The fact that he lived in his own house gave a different quality to his time in the UK than staying in hotels would. The tribunal judge thought that how he spent his leisure time was of less significance. He had in this case failed to demonstrate a sufficient break with the UK.

It's no real surprise in this case that Mr Grace remained UK resident. Looking at the requirement to have shown a distinct break with the UK, it's pretty clear that the substantial periods he was obliged to spend here and the fact that he had a UK property available for his use made it difficult to argue that a definite break from the UK had taken place.

2010 Gaines-Cooper Decision

The Court of Appeal decision in February 2010 in the long-running battle between Robert Gaines-Cooper and HM Revenue & Customs generated a lot of publicity in the popular press.

However, there have been no significant developments since the previous Gaines-Cooper decision or the Grace decision, examined above.

The Court of Appeal decision followed an attempt by Robert Gaines-Cooper to try a different attack. He lost before the Commissioners and the Courts and now wanted a judicial review of the way that HMRC applies its published guidance on non residence.

The decision is interesting but in terms of actually obtaining non residence the position is roughly the same. You need to show that there has been a distinct break from the UK (the Court of Appeal reiterated the same test that was evident in the recent Grace case, as outlined above) and you have to show that you have no substantial ongoing connection with the UK (or as the Court of Appeal put it, you need to ensure that your "centre of gravity" is not in the UK).

What Exactly Did the Court of Appeal Say?

The Court of Appeal looked in detail at HMRC's published guidance on non residence in its IR20 document, which applied up to April 2009 and has now been replaced with HMRC 6 (www.hmrc.gov.uk/cnr/hmrc6.pdf).

IR20 provided for two key ways of becoming non UK resident:

- Going overseas under a full-time contract of employment

- Going abroad for a permanent or indefinite absence (lasting for at least three years)

In this case, Gaines-Cooper was looking at the second option. The Court said that there was a clear distinction between these two options.

To become non-resident by working abroad you have to establish that you left to work abroad full-time and that this continued for at least the entire tax year.

If you claim non residence due to having left permanently or indefinitely, you have to demonstrate a distinct break from former social and family ties within the UK.

The court held that the actual wording of IR20, including terms such as "full-time employment" and "permanent departure", was vague and there would therefore be conflicts between HMRC and taxpayers.

IR20 has been withdrawn post April 2009 and therefore no longer applies. It has been replaced by HMRC 6.

The two key methods of establishing non residence are still included (ie employment and permanent or indefinite absence) but there are now much stricter statements in terms of ensuring that the absence is genuine and that the emigrant has genuinely left the UK.

The Court of Appeal decision is useful because it reiterates the importance of making a distinct break and the importance of not having your centre of vital interests in the UK.

Gaines Cooper has been granted leave to appeal to the Supreme Court, and so we will have to wait for the result of the appeal before we know the final decision in this case.

What Impact Do These Decisions Have?

What these cases imply is that, to become non-resident, you need to clearly establish that your new home and life are in a foreign country and that there has been a distinct break from the UK.

If you want to keep 'one foot in the door' and make regular visits and maintain strong UK ties, this is likely to affect your residence status.

That's why I recommend that anyone who wants to establish non-residence should make only minimal visits to the UK (in particular in the year of departure and in the following year) and UK property should be sold or rented out on a long lease while you are overseas.

A person can also be resident in two countries at the same time. It is therefore not possible to escape UK residence by arguing that you are resident elsewhere.

It is important to note that UK residence is a question of fact and not intention. Therefore, although you may intend to leave before the 183-day limit, if you are forced to remain in the UK as a result of unexpected circumstances, you will nevertheless be regarded as UK resident.

It is also extremely important to point out that many people will, as it happens, be able to establish 'treaty residence' overseas (for example, your typical expat living in Spain or France), due to having a permanent home there.

Treaty residence is determined by double tax treaties (see Chapter 14). It's a way for two countries to agree who has taxing rights over various types of income and gains. It can be a useful back up if you still retain connections with the UK.

2.4   DAYS SPENT IN THE UK

Revenue and Customs confirmed in early 2007 that the days of arrival and departure would not be taken into account when assessing the number of days that you spend in the UK for the purposes of determining your residence status. This tied into their published guidance and meant that there was a certain flexibility in the operation of the requirement not to spend more than 90 days (on average) in the UK in any tax year.

You could, in theory, arrive in the UK on Friday, leave on Sunday and this would only be classed as one day spent in the UK. As from 6th April 2008 this rule is changed and any day when you are in the UK at midnight will be taken into account when looking at your residence status.

This means that if you arrive in the UK on Friday and leave on Sunday evening you will be classed as spending two days in the UK.

There are also provisions to exclude 'transit' days that are spent in the UK from being counted towards the 90 or 183 day limits. These are days that are spent in the UK for the purpose of travelling between two places outside the UK (eg to transfer to a connecting flight).

It is doubtful whether these changes will have a significant impact on many non-residents. It should only seriously affect those who make very frequent visits to the UK. In this case, the new rule could dramatically increase the number of days spent in the UK.

However, sailing too close to the wind when it comes to days spent in the UK, has always been a risky strategy. Although Revenue guidance stated that the days of departure and arrival would not be counted, the courts and certainly the Commissioners stated that they would.

Regular visits back to the UK indicate that you have not made a permanent break with the country, and may result in failure to establish non-UK residence. If you are returning to the UK on only a few occasions, this new rule should simply be factored into your travel plans to ensure you remain well below the 90-day requirement.

In fact, if you look at HMRC's revised guidance in HMRC 6 even they downplay the importance of day counting.

Although there is the new test that states that a day in the UK is one where you are present at midnight, the new version of HMRC 6 states that:

"...This is the general practice, but it will not necessarily be appropriate in all cases. If you spend very significant amounts of the year travelling internationally, you should keep a record both of the days you were present in the UK and of those days where you are here at midnight. Both will be factors when looking at the pattern and purpose of your visits..."

Although HMRC can't simply refuse to apply a statutory test, strictly speaking the statutory rules apply only to the 183-day test and not the 90-day test. HMRC did state that it would apply the legislation consistently in respect of the 90-day test.

This is apparently not the case. When assessing average visits and the 90-day test, there may therefore be a new approach. HMRC may well count every day in which an individual spends any time at all in the UK and use that information to decide whether they are resident.

2.5 STATUTORY RESIDENCE TEST

In the March 2011 Budget it was announced that HMRC will be consulting on a new statutory residence test. This was initially supposed to be implemented from 6th April 2012. However, it has been postponed to allow more time for consultation.

It is now planned to apply from April 2013, although at the time of writing the period of consultation was still running.

Given that the UK residency rules are currently extremely vague, the introduction of a more concrete test for UK residence, laid down in legislation, could make life much easier for anyone wanting to leave the UK.

What Will a Statutory Residence Test Require?

The Government issued a consultation document on the new statutory residence test in 2011. The test should bring some welcome clarity to the law. Of course, there will always be areas where there will be confusion and room for debate but, by and large, the proposed test will take into account a range of key factors when assessing a person's residence.

The proposed test recognises that, to establish non residence, there can be more ties to the UK if there are fewer visits.

The proposed test uses a scale which takes into account different UK ties, the length of UK visits and whether you are a 'leaver' or an 'arriver'.

The Government has stated that to avoid the complexity of current case law:

- The test should not take into account a wide range of connections

- Relevant connections should be simply and clearly defined

- The weight and relevance of each connection should be clear

The proposed test has been designed so that it is harder to become non-resident when leaving the UK after a period of residence than it is to become resident when an individual comes to the UK.

Once an individual has become resident and built up connections with the UK, they should be required to scale back their UK significantly or spend far less time here, or a combination of the two, before they can relinquish residence.

This is consistent with the principle, reflected in case law, that residence should have an adhesive nature.

How the New Statutory Residence Test Operates

There are three main classifications:

- People who will always be non-resident
- People who will always be UK resident
- Others who may be UK resident or may be non resident depending on their UK visits and ties

People Who Are Non-Resident

For UK residents leaving the UK, this classification will mainly apply to anyone leaving the UK to work under a full-time contract overseas.

Under the present guidance they won't need to sever UK ties and will be non resident from the date of departure. This applies providing UK visits are fewer than 90 days during the tax year and no more than 20 days are spent working in the UK during the tax year.

This classification will also apply to anyone who is:

- Not resident in the UK in all of the previous three tax years and present in the UK for fewer than 45 days in the current tax year; or

- Resident in the UK in one or more of the previous three tax years and present in the UK for fewer than 10 days in the current tax year. For long-term UK residents leaving the UK this will therefore mainly apply to anyone going to work overseas

  Once you've established non residence for one year though, if you can then keep UK visits to less than 10 days per tax year there will be no doubt as to your non residence status

People Definitely UK Resident

If the above classification doesn't apply then you will definitely be UK resident if:

- You are present in the UK for 183 days or more in a tax year, or

- You have only one home and that home is in the UK (or you have two or more homes and all of these are in the UK), or

- You carry out full-time work in the UK

This is pretty much in line with the current provisions and isn't any more onerous. This will effectively catch anyone who in reality has their home or job here but tries to argue that they are non-resident.

Having an overseas home will, as always, be an important issue.

People Who Could Be UK Resident or Non-Resident

This classification will apply to most people leaving the UK and seeks to take account of the different ties that people can have to the UK and overseas.

In particular, it reflects the principle that the more time someone spends in the UK, the fewer connections they can have with the UK if they want to be non-resident.

It also incorporates the principle that residence status should adhere more to those who are already resident than to those who are not currently resident.

The Government proposes that the following five connection factors should be relevant to an individual's residence status, but only when linked to the amount of time the person spends in the UK:

- **Family** - the individual's spouse or civil partner or common law equivalent (provided the individual is not separated from them) or minor children are resident in the UK

- **Accommodation** - the individual has accessible accommodation in the UK and makes use of it during the tax year (subject to exclusions for some types of accommodation)

- **Substantive work in the UK** - the individual does substantive work in the UK (but does not work in the UK full-time)

- **UK presence in previous year** - the individual spent 90 days or more in the UK in either of the previous two tax years

- **More time in the UK than in other countries** - the individual spends more days in the UK in the tax year than in any other single country

These connection factors would be combined with days spent in the UK into a 'scale' to determine whether the individual is resident or not.

Leavers

When someone is leaving the UK and was resident in one or more of the three tax years immediately preceding the tax year of departure, the scale of factors to take into account is as follows:

Where he or she spends:

- Fewer than 10 days in the UK, he or she is always non-resident

- 10 to 44 days in the UK, he or she is resident only if four or more factors apply

- 45 to 89 days in the UK, he or she is resident only if three or more factors apply

- 90 to 119 days in the UK, he or she is resident only if two or more factors apply

- 120 to 182 days in the UK, he or she is resident only if one or more factors apply

- 183 days or more in the UK, he or she is always resident

Arrivers

In the case of someone arriving in the UK and who has not been UK resident during the previous three tax years, the scale of factors is more attractive.

Where he or she spends:

- Fewer than 45 days in the UK he/she is always non-resident

- 45-89 days in the UK, he/she is resident only if four factors apply

- 90 to 119 days in the UK, he/she is resident only if three or more factors apply

- 120 to 182 days in the UK, he/she is resident only if two or more factors apply

- 183 days or more in the UK, he/she is always resident

This is a novel system for recognising ties and, for most people who are genuinely leaving the UK, it will probably be welcomed.

The main purpose of the statutory residence test is to combat people looking to artificially avoid being UK resident, whilst retaining strong UK links.

Most people who leave the UK will seek to reduce their UK visits. As such this would reduce their possible UK ties to just one or two from the above list. This is likely to be highly satisfactory and will ensure that, for instance, UK accommodation could be retained in certain cases.

Example

Johnny is a long-term UK resident. He decides to leave the UK permanently at a time when the statutory residence test is in operation (in the proposed form discussed above).

Because Johnny has been UK resident throughout each of the previous three tax years, he will not automatically be non-UK resident when he leaves the UK, unless he is leaving under a full-time contract of employment or spends less than 10 days in the UK during the current tax year. We'll assume that neither of these circumstances apply.

Johnny would not automatically be UK resident either, unless he spent more than 183 days in the UK during the tax year, had his only home(s) in the UK or was working in the UK. Again we'll assume that these circumstances do not apply in Johnny's case.

Whether he is UK resident or not will depend on the type of connections he has to the UK and the number of days he spends in the UK.

Having UK available accommodation is just one factor. Providing he clearly establishes a home overseas, he could retain his UK accommodation, as long as he restricts his other UK connecting factors and his UK visits.

Therefore, if we assume his wife and minor child go overseas with him and he is not planning on carrying out any work in the UK, he would at most have two connecting factors, providing he spends more time in his new overseas country of residence than the UK. This means he could visit the UK for up to 89 days during the tax year without being classed as UK resident.

Note that the new test is planned to apply from April 2013. The consultation period is still running and there are likely to be further changes before its introduction.

The existing regime will apply for 2012/13.

Proposed Anti Avoidance Rule

One very important point mentioned near the end of the consultation document is a proposed anti-avoidance rule that could affect dividends from your own company. Currently if you extract cash as a dividend, as a non-resident it may be free of additional income tax.

However the guidance states:

"...The SRT will include an anti-avoidance rule for some forms of investment income along the lines of the model of the CGT rule described above. In particular, it will apply to dividends paid by closely controlled companies that reflect profits that have built up during a period of residence and which are then taken out during a short period of non-residence..."

There may therefore be a five-year rule for income tax – as applies for capital gains tax purposes – when dividends are paid from a closely controlled company.

2.6   THE IMPORTANCE OF 'ORDINARY RESIDENCE'

Even if you qualify as non-resident you may still fall into the taxman's clutches by being classified as UK ordinarily resident.

There is also no statutory test of ordinary residence. You will be classified as a UK ordinary resident if the UK is your 'normal place of residence'.

On leaving the country you will continue to be regarded as UK ordinary resident unless you go abroad with the intention of taking up permanent residence overseas.

Revenue and Customs normally interprets 'permanent' to mean three years or more.

It is therefore possible to be non-UK resident but UK ordinarily resident. This would occur, for example, where you go abroad for a long holiday and do not return to the UK during a particular tax year. You will continue to be classed as UK ordinary resident until you can show that you have taken up a permanent residence elsewhere.

The consequence of being classed as non-UK ordinary resident (as well as non-resident) is that you will not have to pay UK capital gains tax on your worldwide capital gains.

A person who is UK resident under the 183-day test may not necessarily be UK ordinary resident. Such a person may then claim to pay tax on overseas income that is brought into the UK.

However, a person who is UK resident as a result of the 90-day test would find it difficult to argue that he or she is not also UK ordinary resident and therefore worldwide income would be taxed as it arises, not just when brought into the UK. This is because the visits over a number of tax years would be evidence of an ongoing connection with the UK which would indicate UK ordinary residence status.

One factor that is likely to be taken into account in assessing ordinary residence is whether you continue to own and occupy property in the UK – in particular, where the use or occupation of the property is combined with other factors, such as regular visits to the UK only slightly below the 90-day average. This will be persuasive evidence that you have not taken up a permanent residence elsewhere.

Many of the factors that are looked at when assessing ordinary residence status will now also be looked at when assessing residence status. In particular, the extent of close ties to the UK will be of crucial importance (for example, family, property and employment).

However, subject to this, a person who leaves the UK will cease to be UK ordinary resident if he or she establishes non-UK residence for three consecutive tax years.

2.7   ORDINARY RESIDENCE WHEN COMING TO THE UK

Establishing that you are not ordinarily resident is crucial in terms of avoiding capital gains tax if you are planning on leaving the UK.

However, establishing non UK ordinary residence status is also important for anyone coming to the UK. In particular, an individual who is UK resident but not ordinarily resident can claim the remittance basis of tax and avoid UK tax on overseas income or capital gains by retaining the income or proceeds abroad.

Ordinary residence was looked at in detail in February 2010 in the potentially important case of Andreas Tuczka. Just as the Gaines-Cooper and Grace decisions looked at residence status under common law, the Tuczka case looked at ordinary residence status following a review of the case law.

The position in HMRC 6 (formerly IR20) in respect of ordinary residence status is pretty clear, but it's not legally binding. In this case HMRC pushed for a hearing before the tax tribunal where the strict legal interpretation of ordinary residence was applied rather than the HMRC practice.

What Does the HMRC Guidance Say?

HMRC will class you as ordinarily resident in the UK from the date you arrive, whether to work here or not, if it is clear that you intend to stay for at least three years.

If you don't intend to stay for three years when you first arrive HMRC will treat you as ordinarily resident from the beginning of the tax year after the third anniversary of your arrival.

This means there is usually a three year window in which you can avoid being classed as UK ordinary resident. However, to avoid losing the benefit of this three year period of non UK ordinary residence it is important that you:

• Do not originally intend to stay for at least three years, and

• Do not show any change of intention after you come to the UK, and

• Do not acquire any UK property or sign a lease lasting more than three years

Doing any of these things could result in you being classed as ordinary resident in the UK before the three years are up.

If after you have come to the UK you decide to stay for at least three years from the date of your original arrival, you will be treated as ordinarily resident from:

- The day you arrive if your decision is made in the tax year of arrival, or

- The beginning of the tax year in which you make your decision when this is after the year of arrival

Similarly, if you buy accommodation in the UK after you come here you will be classed as UK ordinary resident from the start of the tax year.

There is an exemption worth noting. If you are treated as ordinarily resident only by virtue of owning or leasing property in the UK and you sell the property and then leave the UK within three years of your arrival, the taxman can treat you as not UK ordinarily resident for your period in the UK.

The Tuczka Case

This case considered the tax position of Dr Andreas Tuczka, an investment banker from Austria. He had arrived in the UK from Austria at the end of June 1997 to take up employment with Warburgs in their London office.

Until May 1998 he lived in rented accommodation in London. In May 1998 he purchased a property there.

Part of his employment duties involved travelling abroad but his base was in London, despite various visits to Austria to keep in touch with his family and friends.

Once he had bought the London flat his work pattern continued in a broadly similar way, although in 2000 he spent more time on projects in Hong Kong and the Far East. His long-term girlfriend remained in the London flat during his business trips abroad.

He accepted that he would be UK ordinary resident after three tax years in the UK but HMRC argued that he was ordinarily resident from 1998/1999.

Looking purely at HMRC published practice it should be noted that the purchase of the flat in 1998 would itself have been an important indicator of ordinary residence status and it was suggested by Tuczka that HMRC clung too tightly to its published practice rather than applying the case law (which he'd hoped would have established him as not ordinarily resident).

What the Tax Tribunal Said in the Tuczka Case

The Tax Tribunal reviewed the previous cases which had touched on ordinary residence and reiterated a number of key guidelines when considering ordinary residence status:

- 'Ordinary Residence' is to be construed in its natural and ordinary meaning as words of common usage in the English language.

- The words are not to be interpreted as comparable with domicile.

- Ordinary residence does not imply an intention to live in a place permanently or indefinitely.

- Unless the statutory framework or legal context requires a different meaning, ordinary residence refers to a person's abode in a particular country which he or she has adopted voluntarily as part of the regular order of his or her life for the time being, whether of short or long duration.

- The mind of the individual is relevant in two (and only two) particular respects. The residence must be voluntarily adopted, and there must be a degree of settled purpose, having sufficient continuity to be described as settled. (A 'settled purpose' exists where there is a fixed object or intention with which the individual is going to be engaged for a long period.)

- The purpose, while settled, may be for a limited period, and common reasons for a choice of regular abode include education, business or profession, employment, health, family, or merely love of the place.

- The test requires objective examination of immediately past events, and not intention or expectation for the future.

These rules were then applied to the facts in the Tuczka case. The key part of the judgement is that Tuczka's residence in the UK was voluntarily adopted, as he chose to come to work in the UK.

The Tax Tribunal then looked at whether there was a settled purpose. In order to do this it didn't look at his long-term future intentions or expectations. Instead it looked back over the period of his stay in the UK and asked whether the purpose appeared to have been settled.

It was decided that the purpose of living in the UK had a sufficient degree of continuity to be described as settled.

Purchase of Flat

The purchase of the flat is interesting. Looking purely at the HMRC practice it would have been a strong indicator of ordinary residence and was presumably one of the key reasons why HMRC initially decided to pursue the case and argue for UK ordinary residence prior to the usual three-year limit.

The Tribunal stated that the purchase of the flat was not 'determinative' in terms of establishing ordinary residence but was an added factor demonstrating that his purpose in living in London for the time being was settled.

It found that even without the purchase of the flat, the evidence showed Dr Tuczka to have become ordinarily resident during 1998-99. This is because he chose to remain in London for a settled purpose, namely his employment, and adopted a pattern of living which continued until 2002 (and after that).

The Tribunal expressly overlooked most of his evidence in terms of his intention to leave the UK prior to three years. Nevertheless, the purchase of the property would be a big indicator of UK ordinary residence. Certainly there is a risk that other foreign nationals working in the UK could be classed as ordinary resident prior to the three year period laid down in HMRC 6, due to having a UK 'settled purpose'. However, we'll need to wait and see whether HMRC pursue this.

Foreign workers should certainly continue to try and avoid purchasing UK property prior to the expiration of the three year period. If they do, they should ensure that the property is sold within this period to stand the best chance of arguing that they are not ordinarily resident in the UK.

Ordinary Residence from April 2013

In the March 2012 Budget it was announced that ordinary residence status will be abolished from April 2013. There were no further details, other than to say that the special relief for non ordinarily resident individuals working overseas will still remain (known as overseas workday relief).

Therefore, from April 2013, there should be no impact of ordinary resident status on capital gains tax.

However, the "old rules"(explained earlier) still apply for the 2012/13 tax year.

2.8   RESIDENCE IN A NUTSHELL

As you can see, residence issues can be fairly complex. It is useful to consolidate the above before looking at the detailed rules:

- An individual who is UK resident/ordinarily resident and domiciled will be liable to UK tax on his/her worldwide income and gains.

- An individual who is UK resident/ordinarily resident but not UK domiciled can claim to be liable to UK tax on overseas income/gains only when the income/proceeds are remitted to the UK. This is known as the remittance basis.

- An individual who is UK resident but not ordinarily resident can also claim to be subject to the remittance basis for overseas income.

- An individual who is non-resident and not ordinarily resident will be liable to UK income tax on UK source income but will be exempt from UK capital gains tax on all assets (whether situated in the UK or overseas), except for assets used in a UK trade.

Example 1

John, who is UK domiciled, has purchased a villa in Spain and intends to spend as much time there as possible.

He stays 10 months in the villa and, in order to supplement his income, rents out his property in the UK through a letting agent on a long lease and obtains a small part-time job in a Spanish vineyard, tasting local wines. He has sold all of his other UK investments and when he's not in the villa makes short trips to the UK to visit family and spends the rest of his time travelling.

From a UK tax perspective he will be regarded as non-UK resident as he has exceeded the 183-day limit and he should be able to argue that he has gone abroad 'permanently'. Therefore:

- *His UK source income (in other words, rental income) will be subject to UK income tax.*
- *His overseas income (his income from his part-time job in Spain) will not be subject to UK taxation.*

If Spanish property prices were to suddenly increase, John may decide to take advantage of this and dispose of his Spanish villa in July 2012 for a healthy profit.

As he has left the UK permanently he should also be able to establish non UK ordinary residence as well as non UK residence. This will mean that his profit from the sale of the Spanish villa will not be subject to UK capital gains tax.

Example 2

Johnny, of Australian domicile, makes regular visits to the UK to visit his friends in London. His visits to the UK over the past few tax years have been as follows:

2009/2010   97 days
2010/2011   110 days
2011/2012   115 days

His annual average visits are (97+110+115)/3 = 107 days.

He will therefore be regarded as UK resident from 6th April 2012 and subject to UK tax on his worldwide income and gains, although he can claim the remittance basis for his overseas income and gains.

If he has investment income in Australia he may not be subject to UK tax if he keeps the income out of the UK and claims the remittance basis. However, to the extent that he brings it into the UK, eg for spending money during his visits, it will be subject to UK tax.

Any amounts that are taxed twice will qualify for double tax relief (see Chapter 9).

It should be noted that if Johnny had any firm intention, beginning with the commencement of his visits to the UK in 2009, that his visits would be on the above basis, then he would be regarded as UK resident from the date that these intentions were formed.

For example, if Johnny had declared in May 2009 that he would be making substantial visits to the UK in the following tax years and, for example, booked time off work to make the visits, he would be regarded as UK resident from this date.

2.9   WHY DOMICILE IS SO IMPORTANT

The concept of domicile is extremely important when it comes to both inheritance tax and overseas tax planning.

It's important to point out that your 'nationality' or 'citizenship' are NOT necessarily the same as your domicile.

You are normally domiciled in the country that you regard as your home – not the place where you happen to be temporarily living. Your domicile is, in a sense, the country that you regard as your true 'homeland' and has frequently been described as the country in which a person intends to die.

It is therefore possible for a person to live in the UK for 40 years yet still remain legally domiciled in another country. Losing your UK domicile is substantially more difficult than losing your UK resident status.

While it is possible to be resident in two countries at the same time, it is only possible to be domiciled in one.

There are three types of domicile:

1. Domicile of Origin

A domicile of origin is acquired when a person is born. Under normal circumstances this is the father's domicile at the date of the child's birth. If the parents are unmarried, it is the mother's domicile that matters.

A domicile of origin continues unless the individual acquires either a domicile of dependency or a domicile of choice (see below). This new domicile will remain in force unless it is abandoned, in which case the domicile of origin is revived.

2. Domicile of Choice

In order to acquire a domicile of choice, a person must voluntarily make a new territory his residence and intend to remain there for the rest of his days – unless and until something occurs to make him change his mind.

Obtaining a domicile of choice is primarily a question of intent. However, once such a domicile has been established it is relatively difficult to abandon. It would be necessary for an individual to cease to reside in the country of choice indefinitely. Later on in this guide we list some practical steps that can be taken to help establish a domicile of choice.

3. Domicile of Dependency

This type of domicile only applies to children under the age of 16. A child's domicile of origin is replaced by a domicile of dependency if there is a change in the father's domicile (mother's domicile in the case of unmarried couples). If this happens, the parent's domicile of choice becomes the child's domicile of dependency. The child keeps this domicile unless the child does not live in the territory and never intends to live there. In this case the child's domicile of origin revives.

Example

John was born in Latvia and is regarded as being of Latvian domicile. John went to live in France and successfully established France as his domicile of choice. His son Jack, who was born in Latvia, would also initially have a Latvian domicile of origin. However, he would 'inherit' his father's French domicile. This would become his domicile of dependency. If Jack intends to permanently return to Latvia on his 18th birthday and makes preparations for this, his domicile will revert to his domicile of origin. The domicile of dependency has essentially been changed – by indicating his intention to return to Latvia, the domicile of origin 'reasserts' itself.

2.10   WATCH OUT FOR THIS INHERITANCE TAX TRAP

Inheritance tax issues are dealt with later in the guide. However it is worth noting now that for inheritance tax purposes only there is the concept of 'deemed domicile'. Individuals are deemed to have a UK domicile:

- If they have been UK resident for 17 out of the last 20 years, or
- They have lost their UK domicile in the last three years.

Example

David was born in France, but has been living in the UK since 1960. He has always intended to return to France, and still regards France as his home. For income tax purposes, and under the general law, David is of French domicile.

However, for inheritance tax purposes, he is deemed UK domicile as he has lived in the UK since 1960 and would therefore have been resident for more than 17 years.

Therefore for inheritance tax purposes, David would be subject to UK inheritance tax on his worldwide estate. On his return to France, David would continue to be deemed UK domicile for inheritance tax purposes for three years after leaving the UK.

Chapter 3

How to Become Non-Resident

3.1 WHAT YOU STAND TO GAIN

Some people emigrate to soak up the sun and live in an exotic location. Others leave the country to escape the UK taxman. However, it is worth noting that tax rates in most industrialised countries are higher than those in the UK. Therefore, if you become non-resident to avoid tax, you may end up jumping out of the frying pan and into the fire!

To achieve a permanent reduction in tax it is often necessary to move to a tax haven or low tax jurisdiction such as Jersey or the Isle of Man.

It should also be noted that a double taxation agreement between the UK and your country of choice could result in your UK income falling outside the scope of UK tax but inside the scope of another country's tax regime. Double taxation agreements are considered in further detail later in the guide.

Before looking at living abroad in further detail, it is useful to remind ourselves of the general rules for income tax, capital gains tax and inheritance tax. The main points can be summarised as follows:

- Income tax is based primarily on residence. If you are resident in the UK, you are normally liable to UK tax on your worldwide income. If you are not resident you could still be liable to UK tax on income arising in the UK, but your non-UK income is outside the scope of UK income tax.

- Capital gains tax depends on both residence and ordinary residence (at least up to 6th April 2013). If you cease to be resident in the UK without also ceasing to be ordinarily resident here, you will remain liable to UK capital gains tax in respect of gains on your worldwide assets. If you cease to be both resident and ordinarily resident, you are outside the scope of UK capital gains tax, even on UK assets, subject to some anti-avoidance rules which we'll look at shortly.

- Inheritance tax is based on domicile. If a person is domiciled in the UK he is liable to UK inheritance tax on his worldwide assets even though he may be both resident and ordinarily resident in another country. If a person is not domiciled here, he is generally liable to inheritance tax on his UK assets only. (The deemed domicile rules outlined earlier should, however, be considered.)

Example 1

Brian is UK resident, ordinarily resident and domiciled during the 2012/13 tax year. He will be liable to UK income tax on his worldwide income, UK capital gains tax on his worldwide gains and UK inheritance tax on his worldwide estate.

Example 2

Peter is UK non-resident and UK non-domiciled. He will still be liable to UK income tax on his UK income, although his overseas income will be outside the scope of UK income tax. On the assumption that he will remain non-resident for at least five complete tax years (see Chapter 5 on capital gains tax), Peter will not be liable to UK capital gains tax on either his UK or overseas gains on assets that he owns when he left the UK. In terms of assets he acquires after leaving the UK, the five year non residence requirement does not usually apply. As he is non-UK domiciled he will be liable to UK inheritance tax on his UK estate – his overseas assets will be outside the scope of UK inheritance tax.

Example 3

David is UK non-resident and non ordinarily resident but UK domiciled. He will be liable to UK income tax on any UK source income, exempt from UK capital gains tax on any gains yet he will still be liable for UK inheritance tax on his worldwide estate.

3.2 CONVINCING THE TAXMAN YOU ARE NON-RESIDENT

Chapter 2 outlined HM Revenue and Customs' rules regarding residence and domicile. While it is vital to understand the basic principles, what most people want to know is how they can become non-resident and reduce their exposure to UK taxes. We will look here at the practical steps that should be taken to help strengthen a claim for non-residence (domicile issues are looked at in detail later).

Selling Your Home

You should consider selling your UK house before leaving the country, assuming that any gain is covered by the Principal Private Residence relief and therefore escapes capital gains tax. If you are unsure whether this relief applies, further advice should be taken.

If the house cannot be sold before departure, you should try not to return to the UK at all until after it has been disposed of and is no longer available for you to use. An alternative to selling the house is to let it. However, care needs to be taken with this – depending on the circumstances, the taxman could argue that keeping property in the UK casts doubt on your intention to leave the country permanently.

This is particularly dangerous where there is a short-term lease, for example under four years, as HMRC could then argue that possession would be obtained within three years of departure. In such circumstances it would be advisable to obtain any evidence that the short-term let was made for commercial reasons and that you intend to be overseas for at least four years.

As stated previously, the taxman could look to see if you have an 'ongoing connection' with the UK or if your 'centre of gravity' is in the UK to determine whether the UK is still really your home. If it is, Revenue could class you as still UK resident. Therefore anything you can do to support the fact that you have a new home overseas (such as selling UK property and limiting UK visits) would be helpful.

Selling your UK property would also be advisable under the new statutory residence test. Having no accommodation available in the UK would reduce the number of ties with the UK – potentially allowing you to spend longer here without being UK resident.

However, it's also worth noting that under the statutory residence proposals, each of the connecting factors has equal relevance. This is a welcome clarification as under the current rules avoiding having UK accommodation is seen by many as being of key importance.

This could therefore allow you to reduce other connecting factors and retain a UK property, whilst still being non-UK resident.

Returning to the UK

You should try to not return to the UK at any time between your departure and the next April 5th – in other words, during the tax year of departure. If you do, HMRC is unlikely to accept that you have left the country permanently until after the last such visit.

You should also try not to return to the UK at any time during the tax year following that in which you emigrate. It would then be unlikely that HMRC could class you as UK resident.

This is important as it shows a firm intention to break with this country and avoids you being classed as having an ongoing connection with the UK. If you wish to visit the UK during your first full tax year abroad it would not be fatal to your emigration claim, but any visits should be as few as possible and for short periods.

If you were to visit for close to three months this is likely to cast doubt on whether you really intended to live permanently abroad. In the Shepherd and Gaines-Cooper cases it was confirmed that you need to break many ties to the UK before you can establish non residence.

HMRC appears to be looking in detail at the position of individuals who claim non-resident status but actually live here for part of the year. They could also argue that you should be regarded as UK *ordinarily resident* and subject to UK capital gains tax on disposals of your worldwide assets.

It is also wise to keep a record of the reasons for the visits to the UK as these can demonstrate that any visits were unconnected with your 'ongoing lifestyle'.

The emigrant should also try to limit visits to the UK in the next two years. Visits during the part year of departure and the three tax years following departure are what will primarily influence the taxman's views on your residence status. If such visits are minimal there are unlikely to be problems.

The days spent in the UK will also have an impact from 2013 under the new statutory residence test. The connection factors directly link into how long an individual can spend in the UK during a tax year before being classed as UK resident.

For example, an individual will be non-UK resident if they spend 90 to 119 days in the UK in a tax year, provided that they are:

- Arrivers with no more than 2 connection factors or
- Leavers with no more than 1 connection factor

You need to be aware that, if an individual spends more than 90 days in the UK during a tax year, this will in itself be a connection factor for the following two tax years, possibly taking the individual over a threshold and making them UK resident.

Example

Jack is a new arriver in 2013/14. He has a UK resident wife and also has accommodation in the UK (ie 2 connection factors). He spends 95 days in the UK in 2013/14 and 45 days in the UK in 2014/15.

He will not be resident in those tax years if he does not work in the UK. If Jack then spends 95 days in the UK in 2015/16, he will become UK resident since he will then have 3 connection factors (family, accommodation and more than 90 days spent in the UK in one of the previous two tax years).

In 2016/17 Jack will no longer be an arriver because he was resident in 2015/16. This means he now has to apply the more stringent tests for leavers. As a leaver with 3 connection factors he will not be able to spend more than 44 days in the UK if he wishes to lose his UK residence.

This example demonstrates that individuals who wish to remain non-UK resident should still spend fewer than 90 days per tax year in the UK, unless they can reduce their other connection factors to a number that will preserve their non-resident status.

Buying a Property Abroad

You should buy or rent a property in another country as soon as possible. This will have an impact on your ordinary residence status as it will show a permanent intention to move abroad. This is probably the single most important action you can take in persuading HMRC that you are not UK ordinary resident.

Many of the above steps are also useful when considering the emigrant's domicile and given the strict line that the taxman is now taking on UK expats establishing non UK residence, many of the indicators of non UK domicile should also be considered in border-line cases.

Making a 'Distinct Break' with the UK

One of the key outcomes of the recent High Court and Court of Appeal decisions on residence is that a prospective emigrant should look to ensure there is a 'distinct break' with the UK. This is essential to establish non UK residence.

Under the previous guidance in IR20, establishing non UK residence was usually thought of as pretty straightforward and providing you met the 90 day and 183 day requirements you had a good chance of establishing non residence.

In the Gaines-Cooper decision HMRC and the Commissioners effectively ignored the guidance in IR20 and looked at an individual's UK and overseas ties based on a review of the facts. They stated that the 90-day limit only applied to individuals who had left the UK. If you were regarded as never having 'left' you could be treated as UK resident even if here for less than 90 days.

The recent Grace case confirmed that in order for a UK resident and ordinarily resident individual to be treated as non-resident and not ordinarily resident, that individual must really have "left" the UK.

When looking at when you have "left" the UK, HMRC will look at the manner in which you order your life before and after your departure from the UK. If before the departure there are clear links with the UK, and these links are minimal after your departure, this would tend to show that you have "left" the UK. This therefore effectively amounts to a "distinct break" test (ie, you need to look for a "distinct break" from the UK).

What amounts to a "distinct break" will vary from individual to individual and no single, universally applicable, rule can be formulated.

What is a Distinct Break?

In one particular case the Special Commissioners helpfully outlined a number of factors they consider to be relevant when determining whether there has been a 'distinct break':

- Whether the individual was employed under the same contract of employment both before and after his purported departure from the UK;

- Whether the individual's duties and place of performance of those duties changed;

- Whether the individual established a permanent residence abroad;

- Whether the individual's partner and family continued to live in the UK in the same family home both before and after his purported departure from the UK;

- Whether the individual did not make special financial arrangements for his time abroad e.g. acquiring overseas bank accounts, credit cards, medical insurance. (In the case in question the individual maintained and used his UK bank accounts and credit cards);

- Whether there were any special arrangements made in relation to your car, driving licence, residence permits, foreign identity card;

- Whether there was any uncertainty about the date of departure from the UK (which they found surprising given that this was meant to be a major event. In particular, in this case the individual did not have his ticket, boarding pass stub or similar evidence of date of departure);

In addition to this, you can also add the following factors when considering whether there has been a distinct break with the UK:

- Whether the individual has items in storage in the UK;

- Whether the individual has club or other memberships in the UK;

- Whether the individual is on the electoral roll in the UK;

- Whether the individual maintains a property in the UK and, if so, whether it is let out, fully furnished and whether all the utilities are connected.

These factors are not in themselves conclusive and must be viewed in the light of all the circumstances.

The result of the recent decisions on residence means that the steps that a prospective emigrant must take in order to become non-UK resident are similar in many respects with those that he must take in order to lose a UK domicile of origin.

In an ideal world to establish non UK residence and show that there has been a 'distinct break' you would therefore need to avoid having any links with the UK and not visit the UK during the first year after your departure from the UK.

The E-Borders Programme

The new E-Borders Programme has been introduced to ensure that information on anyone travelling to or from the UK is retained by the UK border authorities. This will be shared with the Police and HMRC.

The key purpose of this is for immigration purposes, to ensure that the UK Government knows who is coming and going from the country. However, it will have an ancillary benefit in that it will allow HMRC to assess tax residence by keeping track of anyone visiting or leaving the UK.

Under the current rules, if you have left the UK, as a minimum you need to ensure that your return visits are less than 90 days per tax year (on average) and that you don't spend more than 183 days in any one tax year. If you exceed these limits you could be classed as remaining UK resident. Even if you don't exceed these limits you could still be classed as UK resident in certain circumstances.

As well as the length of UK visits, HMRC will also want to take into account the frequency of visits to the UK and any UK ties whilst you are absent. In some cases the UK ties issue is related to the frequency of visits. For instance, if you are trying to establish non UK residence by living abroad but your spouse and children are still living in the UK, it would be likely that you would make frequent visits back to the UK in any case.

You will need to disclose both the number of days spent in the UK as well as the frequency of visits (ie the number of separate occasions you visited the UK) on your UK tax return.

The E-Borders Programme will allow electronic information to be retained (for up to 10 years) and accessed by HMRC.

As one of the stated aims of the E-Borders programme is to: "...help identify those who avoid paying tax by claiming to be resident outside the United Kingdom..." it's fair to say that HMRC will use the information to keep track of visits to the UK.

They have stated that:

"...We will collect the biographical information contained in the section of a passport that can be read by machine. We will also collect details of the service on which a passenger is travelling, for example the flight number. This information is sometimes known as advance passenger information.

We will also collect other passenger information, for example details of reservations and payment. This information will be collected from the carrier not from the passenger. The carrier will be legally required to collect this information and provide it to us as part of the check-in process. Passengers who do not provide the information are unlikely to be allowed to travel.

A number of other countries already collect this type of information, including the United States, Canada, Spain and Australia. The information will be kept for no more than 10 years. It will be protected in keeping with the Data Protection Act and appropriate security controls will ensure it is not used or accessed incorrectly. It will be given only to organisations that are legally authorised to receive it and that need it to carry out their official duties..."

Note that you can't rely on HMRC having access to the information and will still need to maintain your own records with respect to visits to the UK, as usual.

3.3   HOW TO AVOID TIMING TRAPS

Strictly, the decision as to whether you are resident/ordinarily resident needs to be made for an entire tax year. In other words, you are not normally resident for part of a tax year.

Example 1

Keith is present in the UK from 6th April 2012 to 7th October 2012 (185 days). He would be resident in the UK for the entire 2012/13 tax year.

In practice, an exception is made to this rule where a person leaves the UK to take up a 'permanent' residence elsewhere. Such a person is regarded as resident in the UK from 6th April to the date of his departure. In other words, rather than being regarded as UK resident for the whole of the tax year, the individual will be regarded as non-resident for the period that he is overseas.

This treatment is known as 'split year' treatment and is allowed by way of a Revenue and Customs concession. It should be noted that because this is a concession, if large amounts of tax are at stake, it may be unwise to rely too heavily on it.

Example 2

John left the UK permanently on 1st April 2013. He received a large overseas dividend on 3rd April 2013. From a strict legal perspective, John would be UK resident for the whole of the 2012/13 tax year and therefore the dividend would be subject to UK income tax. However, as John has left the UK permanently (and has evidence to support this) the split year treatment would treat John as non-resident for the period 1st April to 5th April and therefore no UK income tax would be due on the overseas income.

In practice, as HMRC is entitled to refuse the benefit of the concession and could tax the dividend, it would be beneficial if possible to arrange for the dividend to be paid in the following tax year, in other words, from 6th April 2013.

The split year treatment is unlikely to be applied for capital gains tax purposes, unless the individual has been UK resident and ordinarily resident for less than four years.

3.4 HOW THE TAXMAN DECIDES RESIDENCE STATUS

When you leave the country you may provisionally be treated as ceasing to be resident and ordinarily resident in the UK from the day of departure – provided you can produce evidence to show that you intend to live permanently abroad for at least three years.

What can be regarded as acceptable evidence clearly depends on the particular facts. If you sell your UK property and purchase a new overseas property, this is suggestive of an intention to live permanently overseas. By contrast, if the UK property remains furnished and not let, this could be regarded as evidence that you have not decided to make a permanent move.

If you cannot produce evidence at the date of departure, Revenue and Customs will normally treat you as remaining UK resident and ordinarily resident. After a period of three years they will review your position in order to make a final decision on whether you ceased to be resident and ordinarily resident in the UK at the date of departure.

They will look closely at the length of any visits to the UK and therefore, even though you may have intended to emigrate permanently, if something subsequently happened to persuade you to resume UK residence, it would be very difficult to persuade the tax authorities that you originally left the UK with the intention of emigrating permanently.

HMRC's approach is to consider an individual's residence/domicile position as part of the tax return. Your claim will therefore either be accepted or looked into further, as with any other entry on your return.

Before you submit your tax return it is possible to obtain an informal review of your status by submitting a form P85 (www.hmrc.gov.uk/cnr/p85.pdf) stating that you regard yourself as non-resident from a certain date.

However, if you receive a self assessment tax return, you would enter details of your non residence on your tax return as part of the normal self assessment process.

3.5   OFFSHORE CHECKLIST

Surely when you move overseas you just buy a new place, move your belongings over and that's it? Well not quite. Moving to another country involves a major lifestyle change and as well as all the personal and family considerations (language, work, schools etc) there are quite a few legal, tax and financial formalities that need sorting out.

I've therefore devised the following simple checklist to help you prepare for a move offshore:

- Review the UK tax consequences of emigrating. In particular, do you have any assets that could produce a capital gains tax bill if you cease to be UK resident (for example, deferred gains on Enterprise Investment Scheme shares)? If you own an overseas company that is controlled by you in the UK, moving overseas could cause the company to be classed as 'migrating' overseas. In this case any capital gains on assets owned by the company would become taxable in the period up to your departure. These are important issues that could mean you have to postpone your emigration plans.

- Review overseas residence/visa and tax implications.

- Consider overseas property purchase or long leasehold. This is important as it helps you demonstrate to HM Revenue & Customs that you have left the UK permanently.

- Choose your departure date. If you leave the UK permanently you can often gain an advantage by leaving part way through the tax year. You'll be UK resident up to the date you depart and non UK resident thereafter. You can offset a full personal allowance (£8,105 for 2012/13) against your UK income, even though you may only fall into the UK tax net for a few months. Note that this 'split year basis' does not usually apply to capital gains tax.

- If you have assets that you want to sell free of capital gains tax, and your new country of residence taxes capital gains, consider a stop over for a short period in a third country. This way you may be able to avoid capital gains tax in both the UK and your new home country.

- Dispose of any assets that you want to be taxed in the UK, for example, if there are significant UK reliefs that would not be available overseas (such as shares or property that qualify for Entrepreneurs Relief).

- Consider transferring assets that have favourable UK tax treatment to close UK family members. For example, premium bond receipts are tax free in the UK but would be taxed in many other countries. You could therefore transfer these to a trusted family member, and they could informally gift you any receipts.

- Review your existing UK connections and end as many of these as possible (for example, unused bank accounts and UK investments).

- If you are keeping a UK sole trader business, and the rate of overseas capital gains tax is low, consider incorporating this into a UK company so that you can sell the shares in the future free of UK CGT. Even if you're non-UK resident you're still within the UK tax net for UK 'business assets'.

  However, if you transfer your business to a company before disposal and then sell the shares in the company, the taxman treats you as selling UK 'investment' assets – which are not subject to UK capital gains tax if you're non-resident.

- Decide what you're going to do with your home in the UK. Will you be selling it or letting it? You will need to bear in mind the overseas tax treatment because although an immediate disposal would be free of UK capital gains tax (being your main residence) a disposal at a future date could be taxed overseas. The fact that you have disposed of or rented out your UK property will also be taken into account by HM Revenue & Customs in assessing your residence status. If you keep the house empty and available for your private use, the taxman is more likely to class you as UK resident.

- When you leave the UK, inform Revenue and Customs of your departure by completing form P85 or enter details on your self assessment return.

- If required inform the overseas tax authorities.

- If you are keeping your job in the UK, check whether your employer has a nil tax (NT) code for your salary.

- Consider the national insurance position if you remain in UK employment. The general rule is that an employer has to pay Class 1 national insurance on salary paid during the first 52 weeks you are working abroad, provided the following three conditions are satisfied:

    1. The employer has a place of business in the UK
    2. You are ordinarily resident in the UK
    3. You were resident in the UK immediately before starting the employment abroad.

If all three conditions are satisfied, Class 1 national insurance may be payable for the first 52 weeks.

- Wait until the tax year after you leave the UK before selling assets free of UK capital gains tax. You can also receive dividends free of income tax in this case (although this may change from April 2013 if the anti-avoidance rules targeting dividends from your own company are introduced).

- If you've been waiting to transfer assets to an offshore company now is the time to do it.

- If you cease trading through your UK company when you left the UK, you can apply to have it struck off the companies register after three months of no trading (assuming the company has no assets). This means you won't have to file dormant company accounts.

- Ideally you should not return to the UK in the tax year after you have emigrated.

- For the next couple of years you should carefully monitor your visits to the UK.

- Ensure you restrict UK visits to less than 90 days and that you have no significant ongoing connection with the UK, to prevent the taxman arguing that you remain UK resident. As we know, in theory you are able to spend up to 90 days in the UK and remain non UK resident. However, given that Revenue will look carefully at the first three years, the fewer days the better, and you should keep a record of the reasons for your visits. If there is a tax treaty between the UK and your new country of residence ensure that you establish treaty residence overseas.

- Complete any self assessment returns sent out by HM Revenue and Customs. If you are non UK resident, are not a UK director or employee and have no UK income or tax liability write to Revenue and Customs and ask them to amend their self assessment records.

- Assets you owned before you left the UK can be sold tax free as a non UK resident. However, you must ensure that you don't obtain UK residence again for five tax years.

- Consider establishing non UK domicile status after you have been outside the UK for three years, provided you have cut your ties with the UK and have made your permanent home overseas.

- If you're non UK domiciled consider transferring UK assets to an offshore company/trust structure to avoid UK inheritance tax.

Chapter 4

How to Avoid UK Income Tax

4.1   INTRODUCTION

The basic rule is that UK residents are taxed on their worldwide income. Non-residents are only taxed on their UK income.

A person leaving the country to avoid income tax needs to remember that the UK, like most countries, claims the right to tax income arising in the UK, irrespective of whether it is earned by a resident or a non-resident.

You also need to take account of double tax treaties. A double tax treaty is an agreement between two countries that determines which country can tax which income, where an individual is a resident of both countries. The rules laid out in these treaties override the domestic tax legislation.

Most double taxation agreements provide for a substantial degree of exemption from UK tax for residents of treaty countries. This means the income is not taxed in the UK but is taxed in the other country. The drawback with this set-up is that most treaties are with countries with tax systems similar to our own – there are very few treaties with tax havens. Double tax treaties are discussed in more detail later in the guide.

So what can you do to minimise your UK income tax bill?

One solution is to dispose of all assets that generate UK income. Such a disposal would also provide evidence of your intention to move abroad permanently and would help to demonstrate that you are not UK ordinarily resident. Of course, the capital gains tax consequences of selling your assets would also have to be considered (see Chapter 5, How to Avoid UK Capital Gains Tax).

If selling your assets is not viable, it is worth noting that, apart from rental income, **most UK investment income received by non-residents is not liable to additional tax beyond what is deducted at source.** Let's take a closer look at the tax treatment of different types of income.

4.2   RENTAL INCOME

Non-residents have to pay tax on rental income from UK properties. There is a 20% withholding tax on the rent. If a firm of letting agents looks after your property, they are responsible for paying the withheld income tax to Revenue and Customs. Where there is no letting agent, it is the responsibility of the tenant. The letting agent/tenant has to account for this basic rate tax each quarter.

Where a tenant's gross rent is less than £100 per week, there is no requirement to deduct tax unless instructed to do so by HMRC.

Any tax withheld is allowed as a credit against your eventual UK tax liability calculated on your self assessment tax return.

Non-residents can also obtain permission to self assess any UK tax liability. This option avoids the withholding tax and is applied for by using form NRL1 (www.hmrc.gov.uk/cnr/nrl1.pdf). Separate forms must be submitted for jointly held properties.

HMRC will generally give its approval provided:

* Your tax affairs are up to date, or
* You do not expect to be liable for any UK tax, or
* You have never had any UK tax obligations.

The tax on the profits of the rental business is then calculated on the self assessment tax return, with any income tax liability usually payable by the 31st January following the end of the tax year.

It is still possible to obtain a deduction for qualifying loan interest as long as it has been incurred 'wholly and exclusively' in relation to the rental income.

4.3   INTEREST & ROYALTIES

Interest and royalties paid overseas from the UK are subject to a 20% withholding tax, with no further liability – **in other words, no higher rate tax is payable.**

50

If you are not ordinarily resident in the UK you can apply to have your interest paid without any tax deducted, by completing a 'not ordinarily resident' declaration (www.hmrc.gov.uk/pdfs/r105.pdf). It should be noted that the interest would still have to be accounted for in the annual tax return.

It may be worthwhile considering whether to transfer any cash in a UK bank account to an overseas account.

There would be no capital gains tax implications (as cash is not a chargeable asset for capital gains tax purposes) and no UK tax would be payable on your interest, provided you are non-resident.

And what about ISAs? Individuals can only make payments into Individual Savings Accounts (ISAs) if they are UK resident and ordinarily resident. So, for example, an individual who works abroad for a complete tax year and is regarded as non-resident will not be able to make ISA contributions during the period of non-residency. However, it's worth holding on to your existing ISAs as you will continue to enjoy the tax benefits no matter how long you live abroad.

There is also a special rule for investments in Government bonds (also known as gilts). Interest from these investments is completely tax free if you are non-resident.

Note that companies have beneficial treatment as a UK company could either make interest and royalty payments to another EU company free of UK withholding tax or claim a repayment of UK tax withheld due to the EU Interest and Royalties Directive. Similarly a UK company receiving interest and royalties from another EU company could receive these free of tax or reclaim the tax withheld thanks to the directive.

4.4   DIVIDENDS

There is no withholding tax on dividends, and for UK tax purposes, there will be no higher rate income tax charge. All dividends are treated as having been subject to a 10% tax charge at source and for non-UK residents, this will satisfy any basic rate income tax liability, so effectively dividend income is tax free in your hands if you're non-UK resident.

Just as for UK residents, the 10% 'deemed' tax credit cannot give rise to a repayment of income tax. However, depending on the terms of any double taxation agreement, income tax may still be payable in the home country.

In the 2007 Budget it was also announced that, from 6th April 2008, a UK resident who receives dividends from an offshore company can reclaim the 10% 'deemed' tax credit. For the 2008 tax year this is restricted as it will only apply where a person owns less than 10% of the offshore company.

However, these restrictions are removed for dividends received after 22 April 2009. Therefore any overseas dividends received by a UK resident will be entitled to the 10% deemed tax credit (providing the company is subject to overseas corporation tax).

So an overseas dividend of £900 paid after April 5 2008 will be 'grossed-up' for UK tax purposes to £1,000 – in other words, giving a tax credit of £100. A basic-rate taxpayer's UK tax bill on the grossed-up foreign dividend will be entirely satisfied by the £100 tax credit; a higher rate taxpayer's liability at 32.5 per cent will be £325 less the £100 tax credit, leaving a £225 liability.

However, this £225 liability could then be reduced by any withholding tax suffered.

The new rules mean that, for the first time, basic rate taxpayers will not have to pay any income tax on overseas dividends.

New Anti-Avoidance Provisions?

As part of the new proposals on statutory residence, some anti-avoidance provisions may be introduced to target shareholders becoming non-resident to extract profits.

The guidance states:

"...The SRT will include an anti-avoidance rule for some forms of investment income along the lines of the model of the CGT rule described above. In particular, it will apply to dividends paid by closely controlled companies that reflect profits that have built up during a period of residence and which are then taken out during a short period of non-residence..."

There may therefore be a five-year rule for income tax – as applies for capital gains tax purposes – when dividends are paid from a controlled company.

4.5   PENSION INCOME

The general rules applying to investment income also apply to pension income.

A UK resident/ordinarily resident and domiciled individual is subject to UK income tax on UK and overseas pensions. However there is one key tax relief. A 10% deduction is given against certain overseas pension receipts. This means that such an individual is only taxed on 90% of his or her pension income.

If the pensioner is non-domiciled and is using the remittance basis to account for overseas income, then the 10% deduction will not be available.

Such a pensioner is fully liable to UK tax on UK pensions but overseas pensions will only be taxed when remitted to the UK, and the 10% deduction is not available.

If you are non-UK resident you will not pay UK tax on any overseas pensions.

If you are a UK expat pensioner who is receiving a UK pension you would usually be subject to UK income tax on your UK pension. However, this is where double tax treaties could come to the rescue. Certain double tax treaties allow UK tax to be avoided and instead allow only the overseas country to levy tax. For example, the UK-Cyprus treaty grants sole taxing rights over UK pensions to Cyprus.

The beauty of this is that Cyprus offers a pension income tax rate of just 5%! This may explain why Cyprus is becoming a popular destination for those wishing to retire abroad. Other countries with sole taxing rights on UK pensions include Australia, Canada and New Zealand.

4.6   PERSONAL ALLOWANCE

The UK income tax personal allowance is extremely valuable. For the 2012/13 tax year the allowance is £8,105 per person, so couples can shelter up to £16,210 of income from UK tax.

Until recently the personal allowance could be claimed by most non-residents and offset against UK income to reduce any UK income tax charge.

However, the ability of non-residents to claim the personal allowance has been significantly reduced since April 2010.

Before April 2010 anyone who was a Commonwealth citizen or who was a resident of a relevant treaty country could claim the UK personal allowance.

However, in the 2009 Budget the Chancellor of the Exchequer announced that claiming a personal allowance solely because you are a Commonwealth citizen was not compliant with the Human Rights Act. The Government has therefore withdrawn the personal allowance entitlement of non-resident individuals who currently qualify solely by virtue of being Commonwealth citizens.

The withdrawal will applies from 6th April 2010 and applies to the:

- Basic and age-related personal allowances
- Married couples allowance
- Blind person's allowance
- Relief for life assurance

There are, however, a number of cases when you can still claim a personal allowance as a non resident. The main one is that you qualify under the terms of a double tax treaty.

What Impact Will This Change Have?

It will only be a cause for concern if you are currently a non-resident Commonwealth citizen, with UK income and do not otherwise qualify. Most double tax treaties will provide for a UK personal allowance if you are treaty resident abroad.

It will therefore mainly affect UK emigrants who live in countries that do not have a tax treaty with the UK such as:

- The Bahamas
- Cameroon
- Costa Rica
- Cook Islands
- Dominica
- Maldives
- Mozambique
- Nauru
- Niue
- St Kitts & Nevis
- St Lucia
- St Vincent & the Grenadines
- Samoa
- Tanzania
- Tonga
- Turks & Caicos Islands
- Vanuatu

Even if you are entitled to claim the UK personal allowance you should in any case consider whether this is worth doing. For most non-residents it's generally worth £1,621 per year in saved tax.

However, to take advantage of the personal allowance you would need to claim it by submitting a UK tax return. This could result in a review of your non-resident status.

If you have limited UK income in some cases it may simply be preferable not to claim the personal allowance and suffer the 20% basic-rate income tax at source.

If a claim is made, this will be dealt with by the Centre for Non Residents. They may take a detailed look at your affairs to determine whether you are truly non-resident. This could prove an inconvenience and the Revenue may also be bound under the terms of an exchange of information treaty to provide details they discover to any overseas tax authorities.

Many non-residents will prefer the additional privacy and reduced disclosure that goes with not claiming the personal allowance.

4.7   MAKING PENSION CONTRIBUTIONS

The tax breaks associated with UK pension contributions are well known. When you make a qualifying contribution you obtain tax relief at the basic rate (currently 20 per cent).

For every £80 you put into a pension scheme this is grossed up by the taxman to £100. If you are a higher-rate taxpayer you can claim a further tax refund of £20 when you submit your tax return.

Your pension investments are then allowed to grow free of income tax and capital gains tax.

That's all very well, but what about UK expats? The good news is that under the pension rules introduced in April 2006, expats can continue to make contributions into a UK personal pension plan.

However, in order to obtain tax relief on your contributions you must either have UK taxable earnings or meet one of the following conditions:

- You must be resident in the UK in the tax year during which the pension contributions are made or,

- You must be UK resident at some time in the five years preceding the UK tax year in which the contributions are paid.

Therefore a long-term expat with no UK earnings would not qualify. In these cases it's worth looking at other saving vehicles.

One option would be to invest in an offshore insurance bond. The investment income and dividends should be tax free and these can be extremely flexible investments. There is no restriction on when cash can be extracted and you can leave the bond to your spouse or family in your will.

4.8   EMPLOYMENT INCOME

Employment income will be taxed differently depending on the residence/domicile status of the employee and where the duties are actually performed. There are three different circumstances under which employment income could be taxed. I'll call these the three 'cases':

Case I

This applies to individuals who are UK resident and ordinarily resident and covers both UK and foreign work duties.

The tax charge is on a receipts basis and the full amount of worldwide emoluments/salary is subject to UK income tax, except for one specific situation that falls within Case III (below).

Case II

This applies to non-resident individuals, or individuals resident but not ordinarily resident in the UK and covers only salary arising from UK duties.

Case III

This applies where an employee is either

- Resident but not ordinarily resident in the UK or

- The employee is UK resident/ordinarily resident but is of foreign domicile, works for a foreign employer and performs all duties outside of the UK.

In either of these cases the overseas salary may be assessed on a remittance basis, and is only subject to UK income tax when received in the UK.

Example

David, of Jamaican domicile, has been working in the UK for a computer company. He is UK resident and will be fully taxed on his employment income under Case I.

Robert is a non-resident, yet he earns a salary as a director of a UK company and pays regular visits to the UK head office during the year (but stays within the 90-day limit and has no other UK ties or property).

He will be subject to income tax on his UK employment income under Case II. As he is non-resident, any overseas income will be exempt from UK income tax.

Peter, UK resident but non-UK domiciled, is to work overseas for four months for an overseas subsidiary of his UK employer.

The duties of the employment will be performed wholly abroad. He can claim to be taxed on his overseas employment income under Case III on a remittance basis – in other words, he is subject to UK tax on income that is brought into the UK. From 6th April 2008, when claiming the remittance basis, Peter may also lose certain UK allowances and could be subject to a £30,000/£50,000 annual tax charge (see Chapter 7).

It is therefore important to understand the definition of UK and overseas duties.

A non-UK resident individual is not subject to UK income tax on salary received for duties performed wholly abroad. Any 'incidental duties' performed in the UK will not create a problem, provided these duties are clearly ancillary or subordinate to the overseas employment, for example going back to the UK for meetings at head office.

Example

Freddy has been offered a secondment to the Paris office of his employer. It is proposed that this is from 4th April 2011 to 3rd April 2013. Freddy is happy with this as he is likely to be regarded as non-resident and not ordinarily resident from the date of his departure. (If you go abroad under a full-time contract of employment you will usually be regarded as non-resident and not ordinarily resident from the date of departure – see Chapter 8.)

Freddy must then look at the duties that he will be undertaking, as it is the earnings from the overseas employment that are exempt from UK income tax.

Let's assume Freddy's job is to source French products that may be in demand from the British market. If as part of his role he is to return to the UK on a monthly basis and produce and advise on the production and marketing of these products, it may be that these duties are not incidental to the overseas employment, particularly if he is to spend, say, one week each month in the UK advising on this. If HMRC successfully argued the case, the employment income would need to be apportioned between UK and overseas income, with the UK income subject to UK income tax.

There were also provisions introduced in the 2008 Budget to provide for a similar apportionment where employee share options were exercised at a profit and part of the employment would qualify under 'case I or II' above.

4.9   UK NATIONAL INSURANCE

This is a tremendously complex area.

If you've been posted abroad by your UK employer you'll need to consider whether you will be subject to UK national insurance on your salary.

This will depend primarily on the status of the country where you are working. For UK purposes the national insurance position depends on whether the country is:

- A European Union (EU) country
- Covered by a reciprocal agreement (ie a treaty)
- Neither of the above

EU Countries

When a person is working in the EU the general rule is that you pay contributions in the country you are working in. This arises from article 42 of the EC Treaty which gives effect to the free movement of workers.

So if you are employed in one country you are subject to the social security provisions of that country, even if you reside in another country (or if the registered office of your employer is situated in another country).

There are, however, provisions that can allow you to be subject to UK national insurance even if working abroad. The conditions that must be satisfied for this to apply are:

- You are sent by the UK employer to undertake work for that employer in the overseas country.

- The work is expected to last less than 24 months at the outset.

- You are not replacing another employee who has completed a tour of duty abroad.

If you meet these conditions you will remain subject to UK national insurance. Your employer will complete form A1 to stop the overseas country applying social security contributions.

If the country you are moving to is not in the EU but is Iceland, Liechtenstein, Norway or Switzerland, there are other (more complex) rules that can apply. Broadly speaking, the legislation of the country of residence applies if the employee pursues a substantial part of their activity in that country.

Reciprocal Agreement Countries

Even if the country you're going to is not in the EU it may be covered by a reciprocal agreement (RA). There are a number of countries outside the EU with which the UK has a contributions reciprocal agreement including:

- Barbados
- Israel
- Mauritius
- Bermuda
- Jamaica
- Philippines
- Canada
- Japan
- Jersey
- Turkey
- Guernsey
- Korea
- USA
- The Isle of Man
- Yugoslavia (including former Republics)

As for EU countries, social security contributions will usually only be paid in one country. As a general rule employees will pay in the country where they work (in other words, overseas).

However, someone sent to work overseas may remain liable for UK Class 1 national insurance if:

- They are employed in the UK, and

- Are posted by that employer to work in another RA country, and

- The posting is for a period not exceeding the maximum posting period allowed by the terms of the RA. The maximum period of posting will depend on the RA country (3 years, 5 years etc).

Other Countries

If the country where you're working is not in the EU and there is no RA you'll be subject to the domestic UK rules.

You'll be liable to pay UK national insurance if you are:

- Resident
- Present (but for any temporary absence), or
- Ordinarily resident in the UK

Note that the fact that anyone ordinarily resident is caught gives this a wide scope. The provisions state that you will continue to pay UK national insurance if:

- Your employer has a place of business in the UK
- You are ordinarily resident in the UK, and
- Immediately before the start of the employment you were resident in the UK.

You'll then continue to be subject to national insurance for 52 weeks from the start of the overseas employment.

So when assessing your national insurance position you should initially look to determine whether you're going to an EU country or not. If you are, the EC provisions will apply and you'll generally be subject to the overseas provisions unless your employer completes a form A1.

4.10   PENSION PLANNING

We take a closer look at working abroad later on. However, where an individual goes to work overseas there are a few issues to bear in mind as regards pensions:

- Will any benefits already accrued in a UK scheme be capable of being transferred into an overseas scheme?

- If you remain a member of a UK scheme, will any employer and employee contributions be taxed/tax deductible?

An individual sent overseas for a long period of service may wish to join a pension fund established in the overseas country.

The pension regime has undergone significant changes since 6th April 2006.

Before 6th April 2006 it was very difficult to transfer your pension overseas but the 'A Day' changes also brought with them 'Qualifying Recognised Overseas Pension Schemes'. These are known as QROPS for short and they now allow UK pensions to be transferred overseas.

Provided a UK pension is transferred to a QROPS it is, in principle, allowed. A QROPS is an overseas pension scheme that meets various criteria and is authorised as a pension scheme overseas. To obtain QROPS status the pension fund needs to meet Revenue reporting requirements for five complete tax years after you've left the UK.

This time limit doesn't apply from the date of the transfer of the pension benefits but rather applies to the date of your move abroad.

What Do I Have to Do to Transfer the Pension?

In order to transfer your pension overseas you need to have left the UK for tax purposes. Therefore you need to lose your UK residence status.

The pension rights can then be transferred to the QROPS tax free and this can be done either before you start taking the retirement benefits or even after you've started receiving payments.

You don't have to establish the pension in the same jurisdiction that you are moving to, so you can choose any offshore tax friendly jurisdiction.

Which Pensions Can Be Transferred?

Most forms of pension can be transferred with the exception of the state pension.

What Are the Tax Benefits?

A UK pension scheme would usually deduct basic rate income tax from any payment. Therefore if you were resident outside the UK you'd need to claim double tax relief for the tax suffered in your country of residence.

If you were resident in a tax haven or weren't otherwise subject to tax on the pension (eg of you were a fiscal nomad and not tax resident in any country) the UK income tax would represent the sole tax charge on your pension income.

Whilst there are double tax treaties that can operate to provide relief from the double tax charge, these would not operate if you were resident in a tax haven or were a fiscal nomad.

This therefore makes the ability to transfer a UK pension to a QROPS very attractive. Essentially it lets you take your pension fund out of the UK tax net.

What Happens After I'm Non-Resident for 5 Tax Years?

After you've been non UK resident for five complete tax years the QROPS reporting requirements stop and the pension fund is subject to the local rules governing pension funds.

As there are some jurisdictions that have no restrictions on allowable investments or how much income you can withdraw this is another advantage of transferring overseas.

If the pension scheme is not a QROPS however, any transfer could be subject to a 40% UK tax charge.

Alternatively, an employee may go abroad to work for a UK resident employer and may decide to retain his UK occupational pension scheme. Again this has been significantly changed by the 2006 pension changes as both UK residents and non-UK residents can now be members of a UK pension scheme.

Therefore you could keep your UK scheme if you go and work overseas. Note that the application of the new pension rules to overseas transfers can be complex and you should take advice from a pensions specialist.

Example

Patrick has been offered an opportunity to work in his UK employer's Milan subsidiary for two years. He has been paying into the employer's occupational pension scheme and wishes to continue doing so. As the employment is expected to last for two years and the overseas employer is part of the UK group, any pension contributions made by Patrick to his UK occupational scheme will be tax deductible.

Where Are the QROPS?

There are many tax neutral and tax-free jurisdictions in the world. The Channel Islands and Luxembourg are typical destinations for QROPS and many financial firms that are household names provide these arrangements. The regulatory and compliance regimes are controlled by the local governments and there are no language or time barriers.

UK pension plans are complex beasts so you should discuss your plan's features with an IFA who understands how QROPS work.

The structure of a QROPS needs to take into account local tax rules to avoid future complications and provide the most tax efficient source of income.

Tax efficiency is best achieved in traditional tax havens such as Monaco but, surprisingly, there is also low income tax in popular destinations such as Spain and Portugal if the QROPS income is structured correctly.

In Spain and Portugal it is possible, with a QROPS, to structure income where 85% is exempt from tax. Also worth mentioning are Malta and Cyprus where favourable income tax treatment also exists.

Tax free cash lump sums, a mainstay of UK Pension benefits, may be treated as a taxable capital payment from a QROPS under the overseas tax rules, so careful planning is essential.

Globally there is a multitude of QROPS – HMRC's current list runs to over 50 pages and is growing. This is a crucial point and awareness of why so many QROPS exist, and the features and benefits of the legislation of each QROPS domicile, is important.

Large numbers of those listed are inaccessible to individual members because they are:

- Occupational schemes of international employers
- Individual and family QROPS
- Only available to individuals who become resident in certain countries, eg Australia

Research of international pension legislation reveals there are many countries which have very different rules and regulations to the UK but have QROPS authorisation and allow non-residents to transfer pension funds into their scheme.

Most importantly their QROPS authorisation does not stipulate that 70% of the fund must be used to provide a lifetime income.

Some of these European and Worldwide QROPS can allow:

- Far greater levels of annual income than QROPS in jurisdictions which adopt and adhere to the UK GAD rates for imposing a lifetime income formula.

- A much wider investment choice (eg to include residential property).

- Access to the fund perhaps via simple fund loans can be achieved even before age 50.

- The complete 100% release of funds to the member.

QROPS into 2011 and 2012

QROPS certainly suffered uncertainty in early 2008 as the interpretation of HMRC guidance notes led to a few QROPS trustees allowing pension fund money to be paid out in full. There was a fair amount of publicity when Singapore was stripped of qualifying status by HMRC.

Guernsey has developed into the primary jurisdiction. The States of Guernsey Income Tax Office recently wrote an open letter to all Guernsey QROPS trustees to ensure they follow the rules correctly, thereby safeguarding the island's relationship with the UK taxman and the jurisdiction's QROPS status.

The Isle of Man has several QROPS trustees and a wealth of experience but remains an unlikely choice as a 15% withholding tax applies to income and there is a possible inheritance tax charge on death.

The most interesting recent development is Luxembourg's emergence as a QROPS jurisdiction, providing robust investor protection in the world's second largest centre for investment funds.

4.11   OUT OF THE FRYING PAN AND INTO THE FIRE

A key problem is that most countries tax individuals on their worldwide income. On obtaining Spanish residence, for example, you would become liable to Spanish income tax on your worldwide income. With Spanish tax rates of up to 56% in some regions, avoiding UK tax is not as big a benefit as it seems!

However, not all countries tax residents on their worldwide income. In Malta, for example, individuals who are of non-Maltese domicile, and who are resident but not ordinarily resident in Malta, pay tax only on income arising in Malta, or income remitted there and this could be at rates as low as 15%. Similarly many of the well known tax havens such as the Bahamas, the Cayman Islands and Monaco don't levy any income taxes at all.

If you seek to minimise income tax, your choice of country of residence is critical. In addition, the terms of any applicable double tax treaty should be examined carefully. Double tax treaties are covered later in the book but it is worthwhile noting that you would be entitled to a 'set off' where tax was suffered in two countries on the same income.

4.12   UK COMPANY OWNERS MOVING OVERSEAS

You may currently be UK resident but intend to become non-resident at some point in the future.

If you also own a UK company you may be wondering what opportunities there are to reduce tax.

One of the key tax planning opportunities is for the company to hold onto as much of its profits as possible, with you only withdrawing enough cash to fully utilise your basic-rate tax band (these dividends will be tax free). Any dividends over the basic-rate tax band would be taxed at an effective rate of 25% (36.1% if you earn over £150,000, falling to 30.6% from April 2013).

If you retain cash in the company and only extract it when you are non-UK resident, you will not be subject to UK income tax. There is also no UK withholding tax on dividends paid overseas. So if you are based in a tax haven or other jurisdiction with favourable tax rates, the money you take out of the company will be tax free.

The tax would then be limited to the corporation tax originally paid by the company on its profits, possibly as little as 20% at present.

Alternatively, you could sell your shares in the company. Non-residents can do this free of UK capital gains tax.

If you are thinking of launching new products or services *before* you become non UK resident, you should think about doing this personally or through a partnership. Then when you leave the UK, and assuming the trade is not classed as a UK trade, the profits generated after you leave will fall outside the UK tax net.

Another option would be to transfer any new products into an offshore company or trust or use the offshore company as a form of recharging company to accumulate profits tax free overseas.

Provided the company is non UK resident it will not be taxed in the UK (because there is no UK trade). If any cash is extracted from the company it would clearly be subject to UK income tax. However, providing the entity is established in a low tax jurisdiction and no cash is extracted until after you become non UK resident, there could be no tax on the company's profits.

Note that we refer to 'new' products here. Any transfer of an existing trade to a new offshore company would be difficult. If the current trade is already making profits it would be likely to have significant value. As such, a transfer from the UK company to an offshore company would crystallise a capital gain which would be subject to corporation tax.

Chapter 5

How to Avoid UK Capital Gains Tax

5.1   INTRODUCTION

In order for an individual to avoid capital gains tax it is usually necessary to remain non-resident for **five complete tax years**. Any gains on assets disposed of during the period of non-residence will then escape UK capital gains tax completely.

It should be noted that this rule only applies if you have been UK resident for at least four of the seven tax years prior to the year of your departure.

If you have not been UK resident for this time, it is still possible to avoid capital gains tax by becoming non-UK resident and non-UK ordinarily resident for the tax year of the disposal (for example, by working abroad under a full-time contract of employment that spans a complete tax year).

If you are subject to the five-year non-residence period and become UK resident within the five-year period, any gains on assets disposed of during your absence from the UK will be subject to tax in the tax year of your return to the UK. The CGT rate for higher-rate taxpayers has increased from 18% to 28% for disposals after 22 June 2010.

5.2   COUNTRIES WITH GENEROUS CGT RULES

It should be noted that the above five-year rule for CGT applies irrespective of what any double tax treaty says. However, you can use double tax treaties to prevent a tax charge *overseas*.

The UK has concluded tax treaties with over 100 states and most of these give the country of residence sole taxing rights over capital gains (except if the gain arises from land or assets used in a permanent establishment).

Therefore you can avoid UK capital gains tax if you move to a country with which the UK has concluded an appropriate double tax treaty. But you may still end up paying tax on your capital gains in the new country.

The key here is to find a treaty country that does not tax capital gains or has a favourable capital gains tax regime. For example, some countries such as South Africa and Australia will rebase the cost of your assets to their current market value and only tax you on gains generated thereafter.

The tax saving potential of this 'immigration at market value' rule should not be underestimated. Essentially it wipes out any existing gain on the asset for tax purposes. Capital gains are generally calculated by subtracting cost from selling price. So the higher the cost (by rebasing to current market value) the lower the capital gain and hence the lower your tax bill.

Example 1

Gerard, a UK resident individual, has built a big investment property portfolio in the UK. The estimated gain after all available reliefs is £800,000. This will result in capital gains tax of about £320,000. If Gerard emigrates to a country with the immigration at market value rule, the cost of the assets would now be their market value. Assuming he plans to stay in this country for at least five complete UK tax years, any sale would not be subject to UK capital gains tax. Any taxation charge in the country of residence would be minimal assuming property prices have not increased rapidly since emigrating. Gerard could therefore save significant amounts of capital gains tax, although the personal upheaval may outweigh the tax benefits.

International Capital Gains Tax Rates

To give you an idea of how other countries tax capital gains, the table on the next page shows a selection of countries and the CGT rates that would generally apply to gains on assets.

International Capital Gains Tax Rates	
	%
Australia	46.5
Belgium	0
Croatia	40
China	20
France	19
Greece	20
Hong Kong	0
Italy	20
Japan	20/39
Russia	13
Netherlands	0
Poland	19
Singapore	0
Spain	21/27
United States	15

However, these are only a simple guide. Taking Australia, for instance, one method to reduce this rate would be to hold on to any asset for at least 12 months. If you do, you would only have to pay capital gains tax on half the gain you've made, which gives a taxpayer paying tax at the top tax rate an effective CGT rate of 23.25%. There are also often separate rates for gains on property, shares or other assets.

Some countries, such as Belgium and New Zealand do not have a general capital gains tax. However, certain gains are taxed as income.

As always there is no substitute for good, up-to-date professional advice. There's no doubt that with the increase in the rate of CGT for UK higher-rate taxpayers to 28%, this will make many overseas jurisdictions look much more attractive.

5.3   EXCEPTIONS TO THE FIVE-YEAR RULE

There are some exceptions to the 'five-year rule' that should be borne in mind:

- It only applies to individuals who go overseas after March 17th 1998. For those who were non-resident prior to this date it is only necessary that they are non-UK resident during the tax year the asset is sold in order for any gains to be tax free. Of course, in practical terms this rule was of most importance in the past, as most individuals who were non-resident on March 17th 1998, would now have been non-resident for five tax years – in other words their gains will be tax free.

- The rule only applies to assets held by the emigrant at the date of departure from the UK. Assets purchased during a tax year of non-residence are not subject to UK capital gains tax, provided you are also non-resident during the tax year they are sold. The requirement for five complete years of non-residence does not come into play in these circumstances.

Example

Peter left the UK in May 2009 and has not returned since this date. He bought a UK property in September 2010. Revenue and Customs accepted that Peter had been non-resident and not ordinarily resident since the date of his departure. If the property is sold in the 2011/12 tax year it would be exempt from UK capital gains tax, as the property was both acquired and disposed of whilst Peter was non-resident. Even if he was to subsequently become UK resident in the 2012/13 tax year, the gain would not be taxable.

Therefore those thinking about investing in property prior to moving overseas could be better off delaying the acquisition until after the move overseas. Provided you sell the property while you are still non-resident, you will pay no tax even if you become UK resident before the expiration of the five-year period.

Note that UK tax legislation is generally subject to the terms of any relevant double tax treaty. Before the 2005 Budget it was possible to avoid the five-year rule by becoming resident in certain countries (for example, Belgium and Portugal to avoid tax on shares and Greece to avoid tax on property). You would then only need to be non-resident during the tax year the asset is sold.

This is no longer the case and the UK tax authorities now reserve the right to tax you if you come back to the UK within five years, irrespective of what any double tax treaty may say.

5.4   TRAPS TO AVOID IN THE YEAR YOU DEPART

Gains accruing on a disposal of assets in the tax year of departure are subject to capital gains tax even though the disposal may only occur after you have left the UK. This is an important trap to avoid.

Example

Paul left the UK on 17 November 2012. It is his intention to remain overseas permanently. He is therefore likely to be given split year treatment and treated as non-resident from 18 November 2012 onwards. He owns a property that has previously been rented out and is keen to dispose of it as soon as possible.

A disposal prior to 6th April 2013 would result in him paying capital gains tax in the 2012/13 tax year.

If Paul were to dispose of the property after 5th April 2013 (in other words, at the beginning of the next tax year) the gain would arise in a tax year in which he was non-resident. Provided he stays non-resident until on or after 6th April 2018, any gain will be completely free of UK capital gains tax.

If Paul were to become UK resident in, say, the 2014/15 tax year, Revenue and Customs will claim the right to tax him and the gain will be taxed in the 2014/2015 tax year.

5.5   OUT OF THE FRYING PAN AND INTO THE FIRE

You need to always look at the overseas tax regime, and how it will apply to both your future income and assets, and your current assets, held at the date of emigration.

We've already looked at situations where assets should be sold after departure to take advantage of the capital gains tax exemption for non-residents, and any uplift in cost to market value.

What about the reverse scenario? It should not always be assumed that UK capital gains tax will be higher than that of the other country. The top rate has been increased to 28% for disposals after 22 June 2010 but is just 18% if you are a basic-rate taxpayer. Furthermore, the annual exemption can shelter the first £10,600 from tax.

In fact there are a number of situations where disposing of assets whilst UK resident would reduce the overall tax charge, including:

- Where a CGT exemption exists such as principal private residence relief (PPR). A disposal whilst UK resident would ensure there was no chargeable gain. However, leaving the disposal until you become non-UK resident could substantially increase the tax charge if the new country of residence is not as favourable. Whilst many countries operate a form of PPR relief, few will deem your last 36 months of ownership as tax free – the UK does!

- Where UK reliefs significantly reduce any gain. The key example here would be Entrepreneurs Relief which applies from April 2008. This can result in a tax rate of 10% on at least part of a capital gain. We've already mentioned the use of Belgium, but if proper tax planning advice was not followed and, for example, shares were disposed of and taxed as income, tax could be payable at rates of up to 50%. The taxpayer would then be much worse off than a disposal whilst UK resident.

- Where the overseas country taxes gains at a much higher rate than the UK. The top UK rate of 28% is relatively high but there are still many countries that levy higher rates. In addition, when other reliefs such as the annual exemption and Entrepreneurs Relief are taken into account, it may be the case that many emigrants (to Spain, for example) will end up paying more tax overseas than when UK resident.

5.6   POSTPONING DISPOSALS AND AVOIDING CGT

An emigrant avoids capital gains tax if a disposal is delayed until the tax year following departure.

Therefore if Paul in the above example needed to postpone the disposal until the 2013/14 tax year, no contract should be entered into until after 5th April 2013.

One key trap to watch out for is that, with the exception of land, Revenue and Customs may contend that there was an oral contract to sell prior to emigration. You should remember this and make sure there is no evidence that would support the taxman's argument.

There are usually two possible methods of postponing a disposal: using conditional contracts and using options.

Conditional Contracts

A disposal under a conditional contract only occurs when the condition is satisfied. A contract is only conditional if:

- The condition is satisfied prior to the contract being 'completed', and

- It is within neither party's direct power to bring it about.

A good example of a conditional contract is a contract that is subject to third party consent, for example the granting of planning permission.

Options

Options can be either call options, whereby the purchaser is entitled to call on the vendor to sell the asset, or put options in terms of which the vendor can require the purchaser to buy the asset. Options can therefore be used to delay the actual contract date, as the contract is not concluded until the option is satisfied.

5.7   AVOIDING CGT ON BUSINESS ASSETS

There is one key exception to the general rule that emigration takes UK assets out of the UK capital gains tax net, namely where a 'branch or agency trade' exists.

A branch or agency trade can exist when any business is being run from the UK. Therefore someone who leaves the country and retains a business and appoints a manager to run it, may find that a branch or agency trade exists.

In addition, a branch/agency trade exists if the emigrant is a partner in a UK partnership with capital gains apportioned between the partners. In this case, gains on UK assets are subject to UK capital gains tax if they are used by either the branch or trade.

A problem therefore arises where an individual operates via an unincorporated business (for example, a sole trader business or partnership). Once the proprietor leaves the country, the business will usually become a branch or agency trade and gains on the business assets will accordingly remain subject to capital gains tax.

There are two common ways around this difficulty:

- Sell the business before you emigrate and reinvest the proceeds in the assets of a new business situated abroad. In these circumstances, roll over relief may be available and the gain arising on the business assets can be effectively rolled over and, as the emigrant remains non-resident, the gain would be completely sheltered.

- Transfer the business to a company prior to leaving the country. If the transfer includes all the assets of the business, the business is a trading business and shares in the company are the sole consideration received by the individual, then the capital gain is rolled over against the cost of the company shares. As the shares are not a business, there will be no branch/agency capital gains tax charge when you sell the shares.

Care must however be taken with the latter method, particularly given the large number of cases coming before the courts regarding anti-avoidance. To avoid attack under anti-avoidance principles, the transfer to the company should take place before the sale is negotiated.

5.8 SALE OF A FORMER HOME

An individual leaving the UK may decide to not dispose of a UK home until after they have left the UK. It should be remembered that there is no UK capital gains tax on the sale of a main residence. As a result, sale of such a property whilst UK resident is still a good option.

On becoming resident in another country, care must be taken as regards the tax liability in the new country of residence, as many countries charge residents capital gains tax on their worldwide disposals.

In such a case, it is necessary to identify whether the UK has a double tax treaty with the country in question as these treaties can determine which country has sole taxing rights. The problem in relation to property is that under the terms of most double tax treaties, 'immovable property' can be taxed in the country where the property is located (in other words, the UK) as well as taxed overseas.

Therefore although no UK liability would arise provided you satisfied the five-year test (in other words, you did not become UK resident within five tax years of the date of departure), the overseas country where you are now resident could potentially tax your gains.

Example

Catriana emigrated to Spain during the 2012/13 tax year. She has purchased a property in Spain and has become a Spanish resident. She still owns a UK property, which has increased in value significantly. She has decided to sell the UK property and needs to know whether there will be any UK or Spanish tax on a disposal of the property.

Under the terms of Article 13(1) of the UK-Spain double tax treaty (see Appendix I), the capital gain arising on the sale of the property can be liable to tax in the country where the property is situated. This is further developed by Article 24(4), which provides that the property will be treated as a UK source, and therefore liable to UK tax.

Since an individual who is neither resident nor ordinarily resident in the UK is exempt from UK capital gains tax (unless the assets are used in connection with a UK trade), the disposal would escape tax altogether in the UK. However, the gain would need to be declared for Spanish tax purposes as the treaty gives taxing rights over land to the country of residence as well as the country where the land is located.

5.9 FAVOURABLE TAX JURISDICTIONS

There are a number of countries that offer favourable tax regimes. Given the complexities involved, and the differing approaches taken by other tax authorities, it is essential that you obtain detailed and specific advice from a suitably qualified tax specialist in the relevant country.

In addition, tax should not be your main consideration when considering a move abroad. Other factors that you should probably consider include political and economic stability, protection of property rights, guarantees against asset expropriation, the level of government regulation, investment concessions, currency restrictions, domestic crime levels, access to quality healthcare, climate, distance from the UK/family, communication and transportation, banking secrecy and ease of obtaining residence.

One of the biggest dangers facing those who move abroad but retain significant UK assets and income is currency movements. The Euro, for example, has gyrated wildly against the Pound since its launch and other currencies behave even more erratically. This can play havoc with your personal financial planning.

It's also critical to avoid substituting a lower tax bill for other financial burdens, such as expensive property and high living costs in your new country of residence.

Some of the countries that offer favourable tax regimes include:

The Cayman Islands

The Cayman Islands impose no taxes other than import duties and stamp duty. In addition, they have no double tax treaties.

Andorra

There are no taxes in Andorra. The only things you have to watch out for are rates and some property transaction taxes. There is no double tax treaty with the UK. It has, however, signed numerous exchange of information treaties with various other countries.

Gibraltar

The main benefit of Gibraltar is that there is no capital gains tax or VAT. Income tax is, however, payable. Individuals pay quite high taxes on their income in Gibraltar unless they can take advantage of 'High Net Worth Individual' status (also known as category 2 status), which is granted to certain wealthy individuals. Income tax is usually payable at rates of up to 40% but High Net Worth Individuals are assessed on only a fraction of their total taxable income.

Cyprus

Cyprus charges both income tax and capital gains tax, although capital gains tax does not apply to profits from the sale of overseas property by non-residents, or to the profits of residents who were non-resident when they purchased the asset. The capital gains tax rate is 20%.

Malta

Individuals who are domiciled and ordinarily resident in Malta pay income tax on their worldwide income. Individuals who are domiciled elsewhere, and who are resident but not ordinarily resident in Malta pay tax at 15% on their income arising in Malta, or remitted there, but not on capital gains.

Monaco

Monaco levies no personal taxes, although there are inheritance and gift taxes, along with business profits tax. VAT is also charged on goods and services.

5.10 USING ENTERPRISE INVESTMENT SCHEMES

A capital gains tax bill can be deferred by reinvesting in Enterprise Investment Scheme shares. The ability to defer capital gains tax by reinvesting in venture capital trusts was scrapped from April 6 2004.

An important point to note is that any relief given to an individual on shares acquired by him (or in certain circumstances his spouse) may be clawed back if the individual ceases to be resident or ordinarily resident in the UK – unless for overseas employment on a short secondment.

Therefore any gains deferred under the Enterprise Investment Scheme will be brought back into the tax net.

Example

Jack sold his investment company and ended up with a taxable capital gain of £500,000. He reinvested this gain in qualifying Enterprise Investment Scheme shares in order to defer paying capital gains tax. He has purchased a property in Majorca and intends to spend significant periods in Spain. Jack needs to be very careful that he does not spend too much time abroad and become UK non-resident. If he does there could be severe consequences:

- *He will be non-resident, so still liable to UK income tax on any UK source income.*

- *He has no overseas income and so will not benefit from the exemption from UK income tax on overseas income.*

- *He will still be ordinarily resident and within the scope of UK capital gains tax.*

- *He will still be UK domiciled and therefore within the scope of UK inheritance tax.*

- *He will have a 'deemed gain' in relation to the gain held over in the tax year of departure (£500,000). Given that his cash is tied up in Enterprise Investment Scheme shares this could cause severe cash flow problems.*

5.11   OFFSHORE INVESTMENTS FOR UK RESIDENTS

What about the typical British person who is both UK resident and UK domiciled – are there any offshore techniques they can use to minimise UK tax?

The first point to bear in mind is that, as a UK resident, you will be taxed on your worldwide income and gains under domestic tax legislation. Therefore, the scope to generate returns in a more tax-efficient manner is limited.

Example

Herbert a UK resident and domiciled individual wants to invest in overseas equities. He decides to invest purely through an offshore broker, and will invest in shares quoted on the US stock market. He will be fully liable to UK capital gains tax on his profits.

However, there are specific exceptions contained within the tax legislation that apply to offshore bonds.

Offshore Bonds

Qualifying offshore bonds allow investors to 'roll up' their returns – this means tax is only paid at the end of the investment period (usually five to 10 years) when the investment is cashed in.

A withdrawal of up to 5% can be taken each year, with tax only payable at the end of the investment period. If you exceed the 5% limit a tax liability is triggered.

It is also possible to switch in and out of different investment funds within an offshore bond wrapper without these transfers being classified as chargeable events for capital gains tax purposes.

Investment in these qualifying offshore bonds can prove highly tax effective. Investments grow virtually tax free within the fund, benefiting from what is known as 'gross roll up'. This means that, rather than an investment being taxed on an ongoing basis, the funds grow without the encumbrance of tax.

Whilst there may be personal tax to pay when the investment is cashed in, proper tax planning, such as arranging your affairs so that you are non-UK resident at the date of encashment, can help reduce this.

Gross roll up can lead to a dramatic increase in the amount of money invested.

Capital gains tax is not levied within the fund on offshore bonds, so an investment may be actively managed focusing solely on the investment considerations rather than being subject, as in the UK, to capital gains tax within the fund.

Savings can often be made with offshore bonds since investors can buy and sell qualifying investments held within the bond without any liability to capital gains tax. Many offshore bond providers offer links to third-party, household name, investment companies, so finding a suitable investment shouldn't be difficult.

However, after the 2008 and 2009 Budgets, HMRC announced changes that will affect when certain offshore funds will be able to benefit from the income tax and gross roll up treatment described above.

These changes are quite technical, and as such it would be advisable to seek confirmation from any potential fund provider whether the chosen fund falls within the above tax rules.

If the fund does not qualify for the gross roll up, the investment would be treated just as any other UK investment. This would eliminate the UK tax benefit as purchases and disposals of the investments or units within the bond would be subject to UK capital gains tax.

Overseas investments, and in particular the taxation of offshore bonds, are a complex area and you should therefore take professional advice when considering your investment strategy.

5.12 MAKING THE MOST OF TAX-FREE CAPITAL GAINS WHILE NON-RESIDENT

While you are non-resident it makes sense to take advantage of the fact that you are exempt from capital gains tax (CGT).

This is particularly the case if you are non-resident (and non ordinarily resident) and thinking about returning to the UK.

After you return to the UK you could be subject to CGT on any asset disposals. Whether you bought the assets when you lived in the UK or overseas is irrelevant.

All that matters is your tax status on the date of sale. When you return to the UK you will fall into the CGT net once again.

Your best bet may be to sell your assets to an external third party in the tax year before you return to the UK. Provided you have met the five year anti-avoidance rule (if it applies) you will then avoid UK CGT.

But what if you don't have time to sell your assets before you return to the UK or if you want to keep hold of them in case they rise in value? Here are a few options:

Transfer to a Family Member

A transfer to a family member for nil consideration (ie, no disposal proceeds) would be a market value transfer for CGT purposes. As such you'd be treated as realising a capital gain which would then be exempt from CGT. The family member in question would then hold the asset at a base cost equivalent to the market value at the date of transfer.

This would therefore eliminate the capital gains tax up to the date of the transfer.

It doesn't matter if the family member is UK resident or not. If they are not they would be exempt from UK CGT in any case. If they are UK resident, they would be subject to CGT on a future disposal but would only be taxed on any uplift in value from the date of transfer.

Note it's important that transfers are not made to a spouse. This would not crystallise a capital gain. Children, parents, grandchildren and other family members would be fine though.

On a future sale, the recipient would only be taxed on any uplift in value (assuming they were UK resident). They could potentially pass the sale proceeds back to the transferor as long as there is evidence that the original transfer was a genuine transfer of the beneficial interest in the property and was not made 'with strings attached' (for example, the original transfer should not be made conditional on the proceeds eventually being returned).

Company

Another option would be to establish a wholly owned company and, say, transfer property into it. A company is a separate legal entity so the capital gain would be crystallised whilst offshore.

One option would be to use a UK company. The company would be UK resident and subject to corporation tax on the uplift in value from the transfer date. The corporation tax rate is likely to be 20%, unless the company is a close investment company in which case it would be 24%. Note that the rates of tax for some UK companies will be reduced from April 2013. Larger companies will see their tax rate reduce by 1% per year until 2014 (at which point the rate will be 22%).

Alternatively, you could transfer the property to an offshore company. An offshore non-resident company is generally exempt from UK tax on capital gains.

This may sound more attractive than using a UK company but the company will only be non-resident if it retains its management and control overseas. If you then become UK resident and control the company from the UK, it will be taxed as a UK company.

To gain any benefit from using a non-resident company you need to ensure that it's controlled from overseas. In most cases this would mean having overseas directors who actually run any business. Of course, in this case there is unlikely to be a business as such and it would be an investment company. It's then even more important to ensure that control is overseas to avoid the Revenue arguing that the company is actually controlled by you in the UK.

Any transfer to the company could be either by way of a gift or for full consideration. The benefit of selling any asset to the company for full consideration is that you can leave the proceeds outstanding on a director's loan account.

Having a loan account with the company can be beneficial when you extract the proceeds in the future. After the company has sold the assets you will probably want to access the cash. You could simply become non-UK resident and extract cash as a tax-free dividend. But if you're UK resident you will be subject to UK tax on any dividend if you're a higher-rate taxpayer.

If, however, you have a loan account, you can extract cash from the company free of tax up to the amount of the loan account. So in this respect a sale by you to the company could be preferable.

5.13 SELL PROPERTY BEFORE OR AFTER RETURNING TO THE UK?

If you are non UK resident and considering returning to live in the UK in the future, you may be trying to decide whether it is best to sell any UK property before or after returning.

Frequently the property will have been the individual's main residence before leaving the UK and was let out whilst abroad. Once you become UK resident again you will be subject to UK capital gains tax (CGT) on all of your disposals thereafter.

You will be able to deduct reliefs such as principal private residence (PPR) relief and the remaining gain will be taxed at 18% if you are a basic-rate taxpayer or 28% if you are a higher-rate taxpayer. Disposals from 6 April 2008 to 22 June 2010 would be simply taxed at a flat rate of 18%.

If you sell when you are non-resident/not ordinarily resident you are exempt from UK CGT on investment assets. However, as we've seen there is a five-year anti-avoidance rule which can tax gains you made when you were non-resident if your time abroad lasts for less than five complete tax years.

This only applies to assets you held when you left the UK. Therefore if you are to avoid CGT by selling as a non-resident it's important that your absence is for five complete tax years.

Example

Assuming you left the UK prior to 5 April 2007 you would be classed as being non-resident for:

2007/2008
2008/2009
2009/2010
2010/2011
2011/2012

Therefore you could return to the UK in 2012/2013 and your disposals made in the intervening years of non residence would be free of CGT.

Usually for UK CGT purposes you are subject to tax if there is a disposal in a tax year in which you are UK resident for part of it. However, Extra Statutory Concession D2 (ESC D2) states that:

"...An individual who comes to live in the United Kingdom and is treated as resident here for any year of assessment from the date of arrival is charged to Capital Gains Tax only in respect of chargeable gains from disposals made after arrival, provided that the individual has not been resident or ordinarily resident in the United Kingdom at any time during the five years of assessment immediately preceding the year of assessment in which he or she arrived in the United Kingdom..."

Therefore you could sell in, say, December 2012, and return to UK residence in January 2013 with the gain still being exempt. There is therefore a definite CGT advantage to selling properties prior to returning to the UK. Note that this applies to UK and overseas property as well as other investment assets (eg shares).

It is planned to replace the above ESC with specific statutory rules that will apply from April 2013.

Selling After Returning to the UK

If you held onto the properties and then became UK resident, you would then need to consider CGT again. Any capital gain would be based on the original acquisition cost of the asset and the fact that you have been non-resident is effectively ignored.

If the property was your main residence at any point you would be able to claim PPR relief. The proportion of the gain that would be exempt from CGT would be calculated as follows:

Period of occupation / Period of ownership

In all cases when calculating the period of occupation the last 36 months of ownership are classed as 'deemed occupation' (ie the property is classed as being occupied by you as a main residence irrespective of whether it has been actually occupied as such). This assumes the property has been your main residence at some point during your period of ownership.

If the property has been rented out since your departure, Private Letting Relief will also be available. This will reduce the capital gain by an amount equal to the lower of:

- The amount of PPR relief
- The gain arising during the letting period
- £40,000

Both a husband and wife (or unmarried partners, if both own the property) are entitled to Private Letting Relief, so up to £80,000 of gains can be sheltered from CGT thanks to this relief.

In many cases PPR Relief, Private Letting Relief and the annual CGT exemption will be enough to reduce your CGT bill to zero.

However, in some cases if you delay a disposal until you are UK resident CGT will be payable (for example, if the period of ownership is long but the period of occupation is not).

In terms of the sale of any *overseas* property after you return to the UK similar considerations would apply. If the property has been your main residence you could sell as a UK resident with the benefit of PPR relief.

Overseas Tax Implications

If you sell a property when you are non-resident you may be able to avoid UK CGT, assuming you have met the five-year non residence requirement. Once you are UK resident any disposal would be within the scope of CGT.

Whether it is best to sell prior to or after returning to the UK will often depend on the overseas tax implications.

For instance if you are resident in a country which does not levy taxes on capital gains, selling whilst non UK resident would usually be beneficial as you could avoid CGT completely.

If, however, the overseas jurisdiction does tax capital gains you may find yourself avoiding UK tax but being taxed heavily overseas. If you had waited until after returning to the UK the combination of PPR relief and Private Letting Relief may well provide for a much smaller capital gain. Therefore it's essential to carefully consider the overseas tax implications.

Chapter 6

How to Avoid Inheritance Tax

6.1   INTRODUCTION

The general rule is that an individual domiciled in the UK will be subject to inheritance tax on his or her *worldwide assets*. Non-UK domiciled individuals are only subject to UK inheritance tax on their *UK assets*.

In order to lose your UK domicile you will need to build up evidence to show that you have abandoned your UK domicile of origin and have acquired a new domicile of choice. In layman's terms, this involves 'cutting your ties' with the UK and establishing a new permanent home overseas. In any case, for expats who are UK 'born and bred', it makes sense to reduce any ongoing connection with the UK as part of the process of establishing residence overseas.

This is something that many who leave the country do not do... with disastrous tax consequences. Frequently they return to the UK on many occasions, keeping within the perceived 90 days a year *income tax* limit. This pattern of behaviour is likely to indicate that you have not abandoned your domicile of origin, with the result that you will be subject to UK inheritance tax on your worldwide assets.

In order to safeguard your overseas estate from inheritance tax, you are likely to have to make some significant changes to your lifestyle in order to produce evidence that you have a new domicile of choice.

6.2   HOW TO LOSE YOUR UK DOMICILE

You should take as many of the following steps as possible to show evidence of an intention to acquire a new domicile of choice:

- Take up nationality in the new country.
- Join clubs and other social organisations in the new country.
- Dispose of UK investments.

- Resign from clubs in the UK.
- Close UK bank accounts.
- Buy an overseas burial plot.
- Avoid subscriptions to British newspapers.
- Dispose of all UK private residences.
- Buy a new residence in the new country.
- Make a will under the laws of the new country.
- Build up a new circle of friends in the new country.
- Avoid retaining directorships in the UK.
- Exercise any vote in the new country.

It should be noted that none of the above factors are in themselves conclusive. However, Revenue and Customs will look at all the factors that can be put in evidence to determine whether there is a real intention to reside permanently in the new country.

Obtaining a non-UK domicile of choice does not protect you completely from UK inheritance tax. You will still be liable to tax on your UK assets. If the value of these assets is less than the nil rate band (currently £325,000) it is probably not worth taking any further action, unless you expect your assets to rise significantly in value.

If you wish to keep significant UK assets, one option would be to place an overseas company between yourself and your assets. What you would then own are shares in an overseas company – a non-UK asset. Care must, however, be taken with the disposal, to ensure that any gain falls outside of the scope of UK capital gains tax. The use of offshore companies is explained in detail later on.

A case to determine domicile status came before the Court of Appeal in 2006. This case actually had nothing to do with tax, rather it focused on how domicile affects someone's will. However, it is equally relevant for UK tax purposes.

The case concerned Mr N who died while living in England. Originally born in Cyprus, he had lived in England for the last 28 years of his life. While living in the UK he established a very successful business and acquired a British passport.

He also retained strong connections with his country of birth and lived in the UK essentially as a Cypriot. He watched Cypriot TV, spoke in Greek with friends, had a Cyprus bank account and sent his daughter to school in Cyprus. He also had two buy-to-let flats in Cyprus.

After he died his fiancée claimed that he was domiciled in England and Wales and that the court had jurisdiction to vary his estate (the case was concerned with how his estate was distributed on his death).

Many who emigrate to the UK will identify with Mr N's circumstances: while living in the UK they still retain a strong bond with their country of birth.

6.3   HOW DOMICILE STATUS IS DETERMINED

As we know there are two main types of domicile (with the third type, domicile of dependency, being a variation on the domicile of choice).

Firstly there is the domicile of origin. This is the domicile an individual acquires when born. Normally it is the father's domicile, although if the parents aren't married it will be the mother's domicile.

Domicile of origin is the default domicile and will continue to apply until it is changed. The main way to change it would be to acquire a domicile of choice. This essentially means that a person would need to show a clear intention to live permanently in a new jurisdiction.

So a foreigner coming to live in the UK could establish a UK domicile of choice that would override the domicile of origin. This would then continue until it is abandoned, in which case the domicile of origin would revive, unless a new domicile of choice was established in another jurisdiction.

It's important to note, however, that overriding your domicile of origin is very difficult and is not something that should be taken lightly.

In this case Mr N clearly had a Cypriot domicile of origin. In order for his fiancée to be successful she would need to show that he had established England as his domicile of choice.

The Court of Appeal stated:

"...the court must look back at the whole of Mr N's life, at what he had done with his life, at what life had done to him and at what were his inferred intentions in order to decide whether he had acquired a domicile of choice in England by the date of his death.."

The court then went on to reiterate that a domicile of origin has an 'adhesive' quality and the burden of proof falls with the person who is arguing for the domicile of choice.

In essence the court looked at evidence to substantiate the fact that Mr N was to live permanently or indefinitely in England and they stated that "clear, cogent and compelling evidence" was required in order to override the domicile of origin.

In this case the Court of Appeal found that Mr N was a non-UK domiciliary, although this was pretty much expected, and is in line with the position prior to the case. The comments of the judges are, however, useful to bear in mind, and it should also be noted that Mr N had no definite intention to eventually return to Cyprus. The fact that he had strong links with Cyprus and the lack of any strong evidence from his fiancée to fix his permanent residence in the UK, seems to have swung the balance in favour of non-UK domicile status.

Based on this court decision, most foreign nationals in similar positions and with strong overseas links should feel more confident in their non-domicile status.

A recent court of appeal case in 2008 (*Henwood v Barlow Clowes International*) reinforced just how close your ties have to be to a country to support a change in domicile. It also made clear that it's just as hard to show a change in your domicile of choice as it is to show a change from a domicile of origin to a domicile of choice.

In either case you would have to show very close ties with a particular jurisdiction. Simply having a strong overseas presence is not, in itself, enough. You need to be able to show that, not only are you resident in a particular country, but also that you intend to live there permanently.

If you do have multiple homes overseas, clearly establishing one as your real home (ie your 'chief residence') would therefore be advisable.

6.4   HOW TO ESTABLISH AN OVERSEAS DOMICILE

In practical terms it is difficult for UK emigrants to convince the UK taxman that they have become non-UK domiciled.

The main way that you would declare that you are non-UK domiciled would be via your UK self assessment tax return.

However, it is only necessary for Revenue and Customs to consider your domicile status if it is immediately relevant in determining your UK income tax or capital gains tax liability. If you are non-resident this will not be an issue, as you will not in any event be subject to UK capital gains tax or income tax on overseas capital gains and income.

For a non-resident, the only impact of non-domicile status is for UK inheritance tax.

You cannot assume that you are non-UK domiciled just because HMRC does not look into the issue during your lifetime. If you wish to determine your domicile status prior to death, there are a few things you can do.

If you're non-UK domiciled and living in the UK, the simplest way to establish non-UK domicile status with the taxman is to ensure that you have a small amount of overseas income that is not fully remitted to the UK.

You can then apply the remittance basis and HMRC would need to look into your circumstances to decide whether you should be taxed on the full interest earned (like a UK domiciliary) or only on the interest actually brought into the UK.

The easiest way to achieve this is to ensure you place some funds in an overseas interest-bearing account and don't remit all the interest generated.

However, non UK domiciliaries (who are also UK resident) are subject to a number of new rules as from 6th April 2008.

We'll look at these shortly, however it suffices to say that using this technique to establish a non UK domicile will only be an option for many provided the income retained overseas is less than £2,000. If it exceeds this, there would then be a whole raft of further tax considerations including the potential loss of personal allowances and an additional £30,000/£50,000 annual tax charge.

The other scenario is where a UK domiciliary emigrates and wants to establish an overseas domicile of choice.

Testing your domicile status in this case is more difficult. One method would be to gift cash or assets (above the £325,000 nil rate band) to a discretionary trust or company. Provided the cash or assets are situated overseas, inheritance tax would be payable unless you have lost your UK domicile. Accordingly, if the taxman does not try and make you pay inheritance tax it will be clear that he accepts that you have acquired a foreign domicile.

In order to do this you would complete a form IHT 100 and also an additional form (Form D31) to enable the Revenue to gather the information they need to consider your domicile status.

6.5   RETAINING YOUR DOMICILE OF ORIGIN

Many UK immigrants and their children are non-UK domiciled. There are substantial tax advantages to be had from retaining this status. In particular:

- Overseas assets can be passed though the family free from UK inheritance tax.

- Overseas assets can be used to generate income offshore. Provided the income is not brought into the UK, there may be no liability to UK taxation.

- There are greater opportunities to use offshore trusts and companies, as many of the anti-avoidance rules apply only in a restricted form to non UK domiciliaries.

As always, however, you and your family need to be careful:

Firstly, the deemed domicile rules (Chapter 2) will deem you to be UK domiciled for inheritance tax purposes, after you've been here for 17 years. Many families will find that their children are subject to UK inheritance tax as a result of this rule. Note, however, that the deemed domicile rule only applies for inheritance tax purposes. Your children could still accumulate assets offshore without paying any UK tax.

The next risk is that the taxman may contend that you or your children have acquired a UK domicile of choice. This is very likely if you have stayed in the UK for a number of years. To establish that you have acquired a UK domicile of choice, the evidence would need to point to the fact that you intend to stay in the UK permanently.

There are a number of other options that could be considered to minimise UK inheritance tax. These are considered elsewhere in the book, however they include:

- Using mortgages/loans to reduce the value of your estate.

- Using an offshore structure to avoid estate taxes.

- For non-domiciliaries, disposing of UK assets and purchasing assets overseas. The capital gains tax implications (both UK and overseas) should be considered, however, for an individual who intends to remain overseas for a significant period, UK CGT would not be an issue, and dependent on the terms of any double tax treaty and domestic tax legislation, there may not in fact be any overseas tax charged.

- Investment in assets that qualify for Business Property Relief (BPR), for example shares in unquoted trading companies and assets used in a trading business.

6.6   MOVING ABROAD TO LOSE UK DEEMED DOMICILE

Many non-domiciled individuals living in the UK will be within the scope of UK inheritance tax (IHT) on the basis that they have the UK as their deemed domicile. This will be the case if they have been resident in the UK for 17 or more of the last 20 tax years.

This is bad news in terms of inheritance tax as it means that their worldwide estate is then subject to UK inheritance tax. This will therefore include overseas assets as well as UK assets.

Deemed UK domicile does not affect income tax or capital gains tax – provided they are still non-domiciled due to not making the

UK their domicile of choice (and having an overseas domicile of origin), they will still be able to claim the remittance basis for income tax and capital gains tax purposes.

Non-doms in this position may consider moving abroad. In that case provided they lose their UK residency and deemed UK domiciled status, they would be exempt from UK IHT on overseas assets.

Note that for inheritance tax it's the tax position of the deceased/donor that is important, not the recipient. Therefore the fact that a non-dom makes a gift of overseas assets to a UK resident and UK domiciled individual would not prevent it being exempt from UK IHT.

Time Taken to Lose UK Deemed Domicile

To avoid inheritance tax the key issue is to ensure that UK residence status is lost.

We've covered this in detail in other sections of the book but you should be able to be classed as non UK resident from the date of departure provided your departure from the UK is genuine and is intended to be on a permanent/indefinite basis or because you are working overseas.

You are deemed to be a UK domiciliary for inheritance tax purposes if:

- You were actually domiciled in the UK within the previous three years.

- You have been resident (for income tax purposes) in the UK in not less than 17 out of the 20 tax years ending with the tax year of gift or death.

Note that the two rules apply different tests. The first rule applies to calendar years, the second applies to tax years.

Therefore if you are a deemed UK domiciliary due to being UK resident for at least 17 of the last 20 tax years, you would need to be non-resident for four tax years in the 20 year period (which ends with the year of any death or gift) to avoid this.

Residence for this purpose is the same as residence for income tax purposes.

Therefore you would need to ensure that your return visits were within the 183 day and 90 day (average) requirements. In the first year, visits should be kept to a minimum to show that you have severed connections with the UK. HMRC often takes a 'qualitative' approach to this.

After you have lost your deemed domicile you could always test your domicile status by making a transfer of overseas assets just above the remaining nil rate band to an offshore trust. Providing you were a non-dom (ie not a deemed UK domiciliary) this would be excluded property for IHT purposes and exempt from IHT. HMRC would then consider and rule on your domicile position.

If you were accepted as a non UK domiciliary from an IHT perspective it would make sense to transfer UK assets abroad to avoid IHT. You could also achieve this by transferring UK assets into an offshore company (owned by you or a trust/settlement created by you).

Chapter 7

The Advantages of Being Non-Domiciled

7.1 NON-UK DOMICILIARIES

Individuals who are UK resident/ordinarily resident but retain a foreign domicile can enjoy preferential tax treatment in a number of respects.

The type of person who can exploit these tax breaks is typically someone who was born outside the UK but currently lives here. Their children are usually also able to take advantage of these tax-planning opportunities.

The main tax benefit is that overseas income and capital gains can be subject to UK income tax and capital gains tax on the 'remittance basis'. This means that tax is paid only when the funds are brought into the UK. This is a fantastic tax break because it means that your investments can grow tax free for many years and potentially indefinitely.

However, there are a number of important changes to the use of the remittance basis, which will apply for income and capital gains arising after 5th April 2008.

In this chapter we'll take a detailed look at the impact of these changes as for many non UK domiciliaries they are of crucial importance. It's worth noting though that these new changes will only affect income tax and capital gains tax.

The inheritance tax position remains exactly the same and inheritance tax, being based on domicile, would not normally apply to overseas assets of non UK domiciliaries.

You would though need to watch out for the 'deemed domicile rules' covered elsewhere in this book as they can result in a non-domiciliary's worldwide estate being subject to inheritance tax if they are UK resident for 17 out of the last 20 years.

7.2   THE REMITTANCE TAX CHARGE EXPLAINED

Before 6th April 2008 if you were UK resident but non UK domiciled (or non ordinarily resident) you could be taxed on overseas income and/or capital gains under the remittance basis of tax. As we've seen this means that you are only taxed on overseas income when you bring it into the UK and on overseas capital gains when you bring the proceeds into the UK.

This led to the development of lots of strategies to sidestep the rules by bringing overseas cash into the UK, without triggering the remittance rules.

The alternative to the remittance basis is the arising basis which is how the vast majority of UK residents are taxed. Under this you're taxed on your worldwide income and capital gains irrespective of whether you keep the income or proceeds overseas or not.

Summary of the New Rules

As from 6th April 2008 if you are entitled to use the remittance basis of tax (for example, if you are a non UK domiciliary) and decide to use it, you will usually now have to claim it in your tax return. This in itself is not a big issue but when you make a claim for the remittance basis of tax there are two key drawbacks:

- Firstly, you will lose certain UK tax allowances.

- Secondly, if you have been UK resident for more than seven of the past ten years you can only claim the remittance basis if you pay an annual £30,000 tax charge.

  From 6th April 2012 this charge rises to £50,000 once you have been UK resident for at least 12 or more of the previous 14 years.

This will have a major impact on whether many non UK domiciliaries will use the remittance basis or not. Some of the key points that you should bear in mind are:

Annual Claim

You can assess on an annual basis whether you want to claim the remittance basis or not. Therefore in each tax year you'll review your position taking account of the overseas income and gains and choose either the remittance or arising basis. If you opt for the remittance basis you'll then need to take account of the loss of UK allowances and whether you'll need to pay the £30,000/£50,000 tax charge (so it would need to be worth your while).

£30,000 Annual Tax Charge

This charge was first announced in the 2007 Pre-Budget Report, however the March 2008 Budget and 2008 Finance Act significantly changed its operation (along with many of the other original proposals).

Crucially the new rules state that the £30,000 charge is to be regarded as a tax on overseas unremitted income or capital gains rather than just a standalone tax charge. It is essentially a 'minimum tax charge' on overseas unremitted income or capital gains. It will however be payable in addition to income tax or capital gains tax on remittances in the year.

What has changed is that you will now need to elect what overseas income or capital gain the £30,000 tax charge relates to. Any future remittance of that income or gain would then not be subject to UK tax again (as it has already been subject to UK tax). You can choose whether the £30,000 tax charge is levied on:

- Unremitted non-UK source income, or

- Unremitted non-UK source capital gains, or

- A combination of these.

The £30,000 tax charge is calculated on the amount of unremitted overseas income or gains that would give rise to a £30,000 liability, after taking into account overseas losses, taxes and allowances.

This certainly complicates matters and now there will be a system of pools and specific rules to keep track of:

- The amount of unremitted overseas income and capital gains which the £30,000 charge has been levied on.

- The amount and type of overseas unremitted income and gains that haven't been taxed.

- The overseas tax on the overseas income and gains.

To prevent you arguing that income that was remitted to the UK was income that had already been subject to the £30,000 tax charge, there are a number of new ordering provisions.

These will treat remittances as being from income or capital gains that haven't been subject to the £30,000 charge since 6 April 2008 (or when you become UK resident if later) before then moving on to the exempt income and gains.

So it's only when you've remitted all of your 'untaxed' overseas income and gains that you'll then be able to remit the 'taxed' income and gains (which will then be tax free in the UK).

Example

If you had overseas income of £100,000 and were taxed at the higher rate you'd need to pay £40,000 income tax under the arising basis. If you retained that income overseas you may decide to claim the remittance basis.

In this case you would need to pay the £30,000 tax charge as well as any tax on any remittances in the tax year. If there were no other remittances in the tax year the remittance basis may therefore be preferred as you'd be saving yourself £10,000 in tax.

You would also elect for the £30,000 to be based on the relevant overseas income. Assuming that this represented the £100,000 of overseas unremitted income (after taking account of foreign taxes etc) you could remit this £100,000 in the future free of UK tax. However this £100,000 could only be remitted once you had remitted all other non taxed income and capital gains (calculated since the first day of UK residency or if later 6 April 2008).

Essentially though you would need to compare the UK tax on the overseas income with the £30,000 tax charge. If it was less you'd be better off opting for the arising basis.

£50,000 Annual Charge

The new £50,000 charge applies from 6th April 2012 for any non UK domiciliaries who have been resident in the UK for at least 12 of the previous 14 tax years. It operates in exactly the same way as the £30,000 charge.

Impact on Domicile Status and Inheritance Tax

There is no change to the domicile rules and no change to the inheritance tax regime for non UK domiciliaries. The changes are to the remittance basis – and not solely to non UK domiciliaries (they therefore also apply to non UK ordinarily resident individuals).

Remitting Previous Income or Gains

If you opt for the arising basis this means that you're subject to tax on all your overseas income and gains – whether brought back to the UK or not.

Strictly if you're taxed on the arising basis you couldn't then be taxed on any remittances of previous years' income or gains (as that income or gain did not arise in the current tax year). However the new rules introduce provisions so that any remittance of previous years income or gains will be taxed whether you're taxed on the arising or remittance basis.

Example

Peter is a UK resident, non UK domiciliary and elects for the remittance basis in 2011/2012. He has overseas unremitted income of £200,000, pays the £30,000 tax charge and retains all his overseas income outside the UK. He will need to also elect for some of the overseas income to have been subject to the £30,000 tax charge.

For 2012/2013 he then sticks with the arising basis as he has no overseas unremitted income. If he remits £10,000 of his income from 2011/2012, that £10,000 will be subject to UK tax in 2012/2013 irrespective of the fact that he is being taxed on the arising basis.

Remittance Basis and Allowances

Anyone who is non UK domiciled or non UK ordinarily resident can opt for the remittance basis. This would need to be via a claim on the new tax return (unless the overseas unremitted income and gains are less than £2,000).

If you make the claim you will then lose the ability to claim your:

- Personal allowance

- Blind person's allowance

- Married couples reductions

- CGT annual exemption

- Tax reductions for life insurance payments

Note that the annual exemption is lost even on UK assets if the remittance basis is claimed.

Low Overseas Income Exemption

There is an exception to the requirement to actually claim the remittance basis of tax. If you have overseas income or capital gains that aren't remitted to the UK of less than £2,000 there is no need to make a claim in your tax return.

In this case you'll be entitled to use the remittance basis automatically if you're non UK domiciled. The benefit is that, as there is no claim, there is also:

- No loss of the above allowances, and

- No requirement to pay the £30,000/£50,000 charge.

When Income and Gains Are Remitted to the UK

The new legislation classes income or gains as remitted to the UK broadly if two conditions are satisfied:

- Cash or other property is brought into the UK for the benefit of a non domiciliary or their 'immediate family'.

- The property that is brought into the UK is (or is derived from) the income or capital gain.

This is also widened to include the case where foreign income or proceeds are used outside the UK to satisfy a debt which is in respect of UK property.

It is therefore a very wide definition of 'remittance' and will catch most methods of bringing cash into the UK including using overseas credit cards, using cheques drawn on overseas banks and bringing physical assets into the UK.

The legislation provides a measure of relief so that money brought into the UK to pay the £30,000/£50,000 charge will not itself be taxable. This is an extension of the 'no tax on tax' principle and is a welcome clarification.

In order to benefit from this rule you will need to avoid the cash actually being paid into your bank. The Revenue will therefore require payment directly to them either via a bank transfer or an overseas cheque.

There's also an art exemption which allows a non UK domiciliary to bring art works into the UK for public display without incurring a charge to tax under the new remittance rules.

As from April 2012 there is a new 'Business Remittance Exemption'. This means that non doms will be able to bring in unremitted income and gains without triggering an income tax or CGT charge, providing the funds are to be used for "commercial investment in UK businesses".

Changes to Overseas 'Alienation' of Assets

One of the key changes in the new provisions are the rules attacking 'alienation' of assets or income overseas.

The original proposals applied where the non domiciliary, or a person connected with them, brought the income or gain into the UK. This was a very wide definition.

However, the 2008 Finance Act has stated that it will now only apply to the non UK domiciliary or 'relevant people' and where they benefit from the overseas income or gain.

We'll look at this in more detail shortly but essentially the new provisions therefore ensure that where overseas income or assets with gains are transferred to certain family members overseas before being remitted to the UK the non-domiciled 'giftor' could be taxed.

There will be a tax charge if amounts received in the UK are derived directly or indirectly from the original income or gains (as they usually will be).

End of Cessation of Source Rule

A popular tax planning 'ruse' for non UK domiciliaries was to rely on the 'cessation of source' rule to remit income free of UK income tax. This relied on the archaic rule that income could not be classed as remitted if the source of that income was not in existence in the tax year it was brought into the UK. This led to non domiciliaries closing bank accounts in one year and remitting the accumulated interest free of income tax in a later tax year.

As from 6th April 2008 the new legislation ends this technique for avoiding remittances. For anyone interested in the 'obituary' for this technique, the relevant extract in the legislation states:

"...(2) For any tax year in which (a) the individual is UK resident, and (b) any of the relevant foreign income is remitted to the United Kingdom, income tax is charged on the full amount of the relevant foreign income so remitted in that year.
(3) Subsection (2) applies whether or not the source of the income exists when the income is remitted..."

Returning to the UK and the Remittance Basis

Anyone who leaves the UK for less than five tax years could also be taxed on unremitted overseas income arising before they left the UK. The income tax charge would arise by treating income they remitted during the years of absence as remitted in the year of return (when it would then be taxed).

There is a separate provision that will charge proceeds from capital gains remitted whilst non resident for less than the five tax year requirement as remitted in the tax year of your return.

Disclosure for Non UK Domiciliaries after 6th April 2008

When the original draft legislation was released there was widespread concern that non UK domiciliaries would be forced to disclose income and capital gains for a number of previous years.

This was not popular as many non UK domiciliaries prize confidentiality just as highly as tax savings. The prospect of having their overseas income and assets disclosed to overseas tax authorities in accordance with the UK's double tax treaty network was a serious bone of contention.

The Revenue released a statement in February 2008 to clarify the disclosure position after 6th April 2008. They said:

"...those using the remittance basis will not be required to make any additional disclosures about their income and gains arising abroad. So long as they declare their remittances to the UK and pay UK tax on them, they will not be required to disclose information on the source of the remittances..."

This was also confirmed in the March 2008 Budget. This provides some reassurance to non UK domiciliaries that they will not need to disclose the source of overseas income and gains. However, if they do claim the remittance basis it is expected that the Revenue could raise an enquiry to gather details of the overseas source in any case.

7.3 PLANNING FOR THE £30,000 TAX CHARGE

Because you can choose whether or not to claim the remittance basis, anyone with no overseas income would clearly not be looking to claim it.

Similarly, anyone with overseas income that was fully remitted to the UK would not usually claim the remittance basis (in order to save themselves the annual £30,000 tax charge).

If a non domiciliary does have overseas income which is to be retained overseas and they have been resident in the UK for eight or more years, they need to weigh up the tax on the overseas income under the arising basis and compare this to the tax charge under the remittance basis, as well as the £30,000 tax charge.

Example

Phillipe is a non UK domiciliary and has been UK resident for more than eight tax years but less than twelve tax years (remember the £30,000 charge only applies after you have been resident in the UK for more than seven tax years, but less than 12 tax years).

He has overseas investment income of £100,000. If he was a higher rate taxpayer and he elected for the arising basis of tax he would pay income tax on this of £40,000. This applies irrespective of the amount of income he actually brings into the UK. However, as he's a non UK domiciliary he has the option of claiming the remittance basis. If he remitted £50,000 of the £100,000 income he would pay income tax only on the £50,000 remitted to the UK.

Therefore his income tax charge would be £20,000. However he would also have to pay the £30,000 annual tax charge which would take his total tax bill to £50,000 (assuming that the remitted income is not used to pay the £30,000 annual tax charge).

Although he would need to allocate some of the overseas unremitted income to the £30,000 tax charge, in this case he would be better off being taxed on the arising basis, paying the £40,000 tax bill and he could then remit all the proceeds with no further tax charge.

If he had remitted none of the income he would again need to compare his position under the arising basis of tax (£40,000) with his position under the remittance basis. In this case the remittance basis would incur no tax charge as there is no income remitted. Although there would still be the £30,000 tax charge to pay, Phillipe may decide to claim the remittance basis and save himself £10,000.

He would then elect the overseas income on which the £30,000 was based and could remit this at some point in the future free of UK tax.

It should also be remembered that if the remittance basis is claimed there is a loss of the personal allowance (and other allowances such as the CGT annual exemption). These would need to be factored into the calculation.

Essentially though, if the UK tax on the overseas income was less than £30,000, you would opt for the arising basis. For example, in terms of tax on income for a higher-rate taxpayer, it would generally only be if unremitted overseas income exceeded £83,105 that it would be worthwhile opting for the remittance basis. This would then compensate for the loss of the personal allowance (£8,105 in 2012/13) and would cover the additional £30,000 tax charge.

If you were a high income earner and taxed at 50% (reducing to 45% from 6 April 2013) you would only need to have foreign unremitted income exceeding £60,000 to make it worthwhile (you would lose the personal allowance in any case due to having income substantially above £100,000).

It is this type of analysis that non UK domiciliaries will need to perform on an annual basis to determine what is the best option. Of course, where the overseas income is large, claiming the remittance basis may be far and away the best option. This will apply particularly to capital gains on overseas assets where large sums can be involved. In this case paying a £30,000 tax charge could represent only a very small proportion of the actual proceeds.

7.4   PLANNING FOR THE £50,000 TAX CHARGE

Exactly the same analysis will apply to the new £50,000 charge, once a non-dom has been UK resident for 12 tax years.

You will therefore have:

- The first 7 years of UK residence where no charge is payable
- The next 5 years of UK residence where £30,000 is payable
- If you remain UK resident you will then have to pay the £50,000 charge.

Of course in all cases you could just opt for the arising basis, pay tax on your worldwide income and avoid any remittance charge.

Once you have to pay the £50,000 remittance basis charge, your break-even point will obviously change significantly.

If you have just overseas capital gains, the break-even point as a higher-rate taxpayer would be £178,571:

$$£178,571 \times 28\% = £50,000$$

In addition, when you add the £10,600 annual CGT exemption, the minimum overseas gain you would need before it is worth paying the £50,000 tax charge would be £189,171.

If you have no other taxable income, any capital gains are taxed at 18% up to £34,370 (the basic-rate band for the 2012/13 tax year). Above this they are taxed at 28%.

In this case, you would need to have unremitted gains of at least £201,445 before it would be worthwhile claiming the remittance basis and paying the £50,000 tax charge.

If you have unremitted income, it's likely that you would be paying income tax at the additional rate (50% for 2012/13) on at least part of your income before it would make sense to claim the remittance basis and pay the £50,000 tax charge. Of course, if all your income was taxed at 50% you would need to have £100,000 of unremitted income before it would be worthwhile.

If there was no other UK income then you would need to have unremitted income of around £142,200 before claiming the remittance basis and paying the £50,000 charge made sense.

Of course the good thing about the remittance provisions is that you can swap between the remittance basis and arising basis as you please.

Therefore even with over 12 years of UK residence, just one year of exceptional foreign income or capital gains could make claiming the remittance basis worthwhile.

7.5   CAPITAL & INCOME ACCOUNTS

Traditionally non UK domiciliaries have been advised to use separate capital and income accounts to maximise the benefit of the remittance rules.

In this case at least three overseas bank accounts would be used:

• The first account for your existing capital.
• The second account to deposit the proceeds of any asset disposals.
• The third account to contain the interest from the first two accounts, along with any other foreign source income.

The point of this exercise is to segregate your foreign income and gains.

If you want to bring money into the country you should first remit funds from the first bank account. This can usually be done tax free.

If further funds are required, then withdrawals can be made from the second account, which would effectively subject the withdrawals to capital gains tax. Finally, withdrawals from the third account would be subject to income tax.

Another advantage of utilising these accounts is that, for inheritance tax purposes, the foreign bank accounts of a non-UK domiciliary will usually be outside the scope of UK inheritance tax.

Example

Hercule, who was born in Belgium, has been offered a contract of employment with a UK company. It is envisaged that he will be in the UK for five years before returning to Belgium.

Hercule has significant assets in France and has decided to dispose of his main residence before he commences his UK employment. Any proceeds of this sale should be put into overseas account 1. After the commencement of his contract, he hears that the Belgian property market is about to collapse and he decides to sell his other Belgian property. If he claims the remittance basis the proceeds of this sale should go into overseas account 2. Any overseas income that he earns, for example rental income from his properties or interest on his overseas bank accounts should be deposited in overseas account 3 if he's claiming the remittance basis. (If he was not claiming the remittance basis there would be no benefit in separating the income or proceeds other than making it easier to identify income and capital gains).

Hercule may never need to use any of his foreign income/proceeds during his period of stay in the UK, in which case none of the foreign income/gains would be taxable. If he does require any funds they should be remitted in the following order:

- ***Account 1** – Not subject to UK capital gains tax as the assets were disposed of before Hercule was UK resident.*

- ***Account 2** – Subject to UK capital gains tax on the remittance basis, as the disposal occurred while Hercule was UK resident but non-domiciled and the remittance basis was claimed. Capital gains tax is usually preferable to income tax as there are more reliefs available.*

- ***Account 3** – Subject to UK income tax on the remittance basis as overseas income of a UK resident/non-domiciliary.*

After the 2008 tax changes, splitting out income and capital is still advisable in any case, if only for ease of reporting. Any capital acquired before you became UK resident or that represented gifts or inheritances from family members should be remittable to the UK free of any tax charges even under the new rules (in other words even on the arising basis it wouldn't be subject to tax).

However, any income generated on this credited to a separate income account would be subject to UK tax if the arising basis was adopted. You could claim the remittance basis on this but this would only be advisable if either the income was large or there was other unremitted income or gains which offset the £30,000/£50,000 tax charge.

7.6   MARRIED COUPLES

The £30,000/£50,000 annual tax charge for anyone that claims the remittance basis could mean that married couples need to undertake some careful tax planning in respect of their overseas assets.

Under these rules a non domiciliary with overseas income has two choices:

- Claim the arising basis and pay tax in the UK on the overseas income as it arises.

- Claim the remittance basis, pay the £30,000/£50,000 tax charge and only pay tax on overseas income remitted to the UK.

If a married couple hold overseas income producing assets jointly they could choose the arising basis, with each person being taxed in the UK on half of the overseas income, or they could each claim the remittance basis (assuming they're both non UK domiciliaries), pay a double £30,000/£50,000 tax charge (one each) and only be taxed on their remittances.

This double tax charge for the remittances raises the breakeven point for married non UK domiciliaries significantly.

Another option would be for one to opt for the remittance basis, retain income abroad and pay the £30,000/£50,000 charge. The other could then opt for the arising basis and bring their share of the income into the UK.

In cases where some of the income is to be retained abroad this is likely to be a good option, unless the overseas income generated is very substantial.

The other option would be to transfer the overseas assets into the name of one of the spouses. This would then allow the remittance basis to be claimed and only one £30,000/£50,000 tax charge to be levied. This may be the preferred option if the overseas income is substantial and does not need to be remitted back to the UK.

7.7   RESIDENCE

The £30,000 charge will only apply where you have been resident in the UK for more than seven tax years (in other words, eight or more tax years) out of the past ten tax years.

The £50,000 applies from 6th April 2012 to any non UK domiciliaries who have been resident in the UK for at least 12 of the previous 14 tax years.

This will therefore make your residence status crucially important.

In addition it doesn't apply just to complete tax years. Where there are any 'split years' of UK residence they will count them towards the seven year limit.

So if you arrived in the UK in June 2012 and were classed as resident from that point, tax year 2012/13 would be classed as a year of residence when assessing whether or not you are subject to the £30,000/£50,000 annual tax charge.

7.8   INCOME-FREE INVESTMENTS

You could hold overseas investments that don't provide income but instead provide a capital return on disposal or redemption.

You could therefore simply claim the arising basis whilst UK resident which would avoid the £30,000/£50,000 tax charge and ensure there was no direct income tax or capital gains tax charge (as there would be no income or gain). You could then crystallise the capital gain when non resident.

This could include using offshore funds or simply overseas shares or investments with a low dividend yield or income return. These types of investments are likely to prove popular with UK non domiciliaries.

7.9 THE NEW REMITTANCE TAX RULES – FAQS

Will I Have to Pay The £30,000/£50,000 Tax Charge If I'm A Non UK Domiciliary?

Not necessarily. This is not a charge on non domicile status but rather a minimum tax charge on non UK domiciliaries where they have overseas income and gains that aren't brought back to the UK.

You'll only have to pay the £30,000 tax charge if you are:

- a non UK domiciliary

- who has lived in the UK for more than 7 of the last 10 tax years

- and who claims the remittance basis.

If you don't claim the remittance basis or haven't lived here for the 7 year period, you won't have to pay the £30,000 tax charge.

Similarly, the £50,000 charge only applies to non UK domiciliaries who have been resident in the UK for at least 12 of the previous 14 tax years and who claim the remittance basis.

It's also worth noting that anyone under 18 years of age doesn't have to pay the £30,000/£50,000 tax charge.

If I Want to Use The Remittance Basis Will I Always Have to Claim It?

Usually yes. It is usually only if you have unremitted overseas income or gains of less than £2,000 that no claim will be necessary.

In this case the remittance basis will apply automatically and the income/gains of up to £2,000 can be retained overseas free of UK tax without suffering the £30,000/£50,000 annual charge or the loss of UK allowances.

The provisions will also be extended to ensure that the remittance basis applies automatically where a non-dom has total UK income or gains of no more than £100 which have been taxed in the UK, provided they make no remittances to the UK in that tax year.

How Will I Claim The Remittance Basis?

If you do want to claim the remittance basis of tax you will need to complete a section in the residence and remittance pages on your tax return.

Will I Always Lose My Personal Allowance/Annual Exemption?

If you claim the remittance basis you will usually lose the personal allowance (including the blind person's allowance) and the CGT annual exemption.

There is an exception to this where the unremitted overseas income or gains are less than £2,000. In this case the allowances won't be lost.

Does The Loss Of The Annual Exemption Only Apply to Overseas Gains?

If you do claim the remittance basis and lose the annual exemption it will not be available for offset against UK or overseas gains.

I Have Overseas Income - Should I Claim The Remittance Basis or Not?

Generally speaking if you are subject to the £30,000 tax charge, are a higher-rate taxpayer and the overseas unremitted income is less than £83,105, it may be worthwhile sticking with the arising basis in 2012/13. In this case the UK tax on the overseas income (less the tax saving from being able to use the UK personal allowance) will be less than the minimum £30,000 tax charge payable if you claimed the remittance basis.

Can I Still Avoid Remitting Income by Gifting Cash to Family Overseas?

The legislation has clamped down on this practice. In the past it used to be possible to gift cash to family members overseas who would then bring the cash into the UK.

The new legislation looks to class this as a remittance if the transfer into the UK was by or for the benefit of your immediate family. This includes your spouse or civil partner, unmarried partners and children and grandchildren under the age of 18.

If you wanted to use this technique now you would need to transfer to family members who aren't caught by this definition and ensure that you or your immediate family (or connected companies or trusts) could not benefit from the transfer.

Is It Still Worth Having Capital and Income Accounts?

Yes it is, if you are or may opt for the remittance basis in the future (and pay the £30,000/£50,000 annual charge).

If you're opting for the arising basis all income or gains in that year would be taxed and the capital/income accounts would have no impact on this other than making reporting easier.

Any income credited to the income account would be taxed as would any capital gains in the capital account.

If you were taxed on the arising basis and could use the remittance basis in the future it would be advisable to keep UK taxed income or gains out of the overseas capital and income accounts to avoid mixing up taxed overseas income or gains with unremitted and untaxed overseas income or gains.

Can Pre-existing Capital Still Be Brought Into The UK Free of Tax?

Yes it should be and this should be kept in a separate account.

Can I Avoid The £30,000/£50,000 Tax Charge by Losing UK Residence?

Yes. You can use the remittance basis without paying the £30,000 annual tax charge until you have been UK resident for more than 7 in the past 10 tax years.

Once you exceed this you'll need to either stop using the remittance basis or pay the £30,000 in addition to tax on anything remitted (other than to pay the £30,000 tax charge).

The £50,000 charge kicks in from April 2012 once you have been UK resident for 12 tax years or more out of the last 14.

Is Non UK Domicile Status Still Beneficial for Tax Purposes?

Yes. It has numerous inheritance tax advantages as well as allowing the option of claiming the remittance basis. There is also the option of retaining income or gains of up to £2,000 per tax year overseas free of UK tax.

Can I Use Reinvested or Deferred Overseas Income to Avoid Paying UK Tax?

Yes you can. If you invest in overseas investments with a low income yield there would be no income to tax and the arising basis could be used, saving the £30,000/£50,000 tax charge.

Providing the income was below £2,000 the remittance basis could even be used to retain the income overseas without it being taxed.

The investments could then be sold free of CGT after departure from the UK.

7.10   GIFTING ASSETS ABROAD TO AVOID THE REMITTANCE RULES

In the past a common method for non UK domiciliaries to avoid the remittance rules was to gift overseas assets to a family member who could then bring the asset into the UK. The remittance basis effectively states that income and capital gains from overseas assets are only taxed to the extent that the overseas income or proceeds are brought into the UK.

By transferring the asset to a third party, who then brought it into the UK, this ensured that the non domiciliary had not made any remittance so there would be no UK tax on the income or gains remitted. In order for this to be successful, it was essential that:

- The transfer was a genuine transfer and was made 'with no strings attached'. Therefore there would need to be legal documentation evidencing the transfer (eg a deed of gift) with the giftee having full legal and beneficial ownership.

- The transfer was made overseas. If there was any argument that an agreement was made in the UK for the transfer the Revenue could argue that there was a remittance by the non domiciliary.

The new legislation which applies from 6th April 2008 has tightened up this rule but there are still lots of opportunities. It will class income or gains as remitted to the UK broadly if two conditions are satisfied.

- Cash or other property is brought into the UK for the benefit of the non domiciliary or 'relevant persons'.

- The property that is brought back to the UK is (or is derived from) the income or capital gain .

This is also widened to include the case where foreign income/proceeds are used outside the UK to satisfy a debt which is in respect of UK property (this therefore combats a non domiciliary obtaining an overseas loan, spending the funds in the UK, and then clearing the debt with overseas income or gains).

Of key importance in the new provisions is the fact that income or gains are classed as remitted not only if they're brought back by the non domiciliary, but also if they're brought back into the UK for the benefit of any 'relevant people'.

So the overseas gift would still be caught by these rules if you transferred to a person overseas who wasn't a 'relevant person' if any relevant person could actually benefit when the gift was brought back into the UK. For instance, if you gifted overseas cash to your niece, although this is not a transfer to a 'relevant person', if she later used the cash to buy you a new car in the UK or to pay some of your UK bills this would still be classed as a remittance.

Who Are Relevant People?

The definition of 'relevant people' includes:

- The non domiciliary

- Their spouse or civil partner

- Their partner if they're unmarried, provided they are living together as though they were married or in a civil partnership.

- Their children and grandchildren aged under 18

Unmarried couples aren't usually caught within these definitions, but they are for this purpose.

There are still a number of family relationships that aren't caught by the new remittance tax rules.

These include:

- Adult children
- Adult grandchildren
- Uncles
- Aunts
- Brothers
- Sisters
- Nephews
- Nieces
- Cousins
- Separated couples
- Divorced couples

In addition, close friends wouldn't fall within these rules.

Trustees

Relevant people also includes trusts where any of the individuals caught by the provisions above (spouses, minor grandchildren etc) are a settlor or beneficiary.

Therefore simply transferring overseas assets to a trust you set up wouldn't avoid the remittance provisions if the gains were remitted back to the UK.

If you are thinking of gifting cash or other assets overseas before having them remitted to the UK, it's important to ensure that the transfer is not to a 'relevant person' and that no relevant person can benefit from the gifted assets. The best option here would be to use family or close friends who do not fall into the definition of relevant person.

7.11 HOW THE REMITTANCE BASIS APPLIES TO OVERSEAS GAINS

As stated above, capital gains in respect of assets situated outside the UK can be taxable on the remittance basis if a non domiciliary makes the necessary claim. Any capital losses are not usually allowable.

However, the 2008 Finance Act introduced provisions so that if the arising basis is chosen, overseas capital losses can be offset as normal against other capital gains. The caveat here is that the remittance basis must not be claimed at all to get relief for the losses.

There is also a new regime that allows non domiciliaries to elect for foreign losses to be offset against capital gains (both UK and overseas) even though they're using the remittance basis. These are complex provisions which we've looked at in detail in our non-domicile tax guide: *Tax Saving Tactics For Non-Doms*.

In terms of capital gains where the overseas gain is significant, the tax saved by retaining proceeds abroad could easily outweigh the £30,000/£50,000 tax charge for using the remittance basis.

120

Example

Steve, a non-UK domiciliary, has been living in the UK for eight years and is therefore classed as UK resident. He has overseas assets that originally cost him £1,000,000 and he is planning to sell them for £1,500,000.

If Steve claims the remittance basis the gain of £500,000 (less any reliefs) will not be subject to UK capital gains tax – provided the proceeds of £1,500,000 are not brought into the country, for example, deposited in a UK bank account or used to settle UK debts.

If only part of the proceeds is remitted, then based on the legislation and Revenue guidance, the remittance is first classed as capital gain before underlying capital. For example, if £150,000 of proceeds is remitted to the UK, this would all be taxable. Of course, any tax payable on the remittance is in addition to the £30,000 remittance tax charge.

7.12   BUYING PROPERTY OVERSEAS

For those who are UK resident and ordinarily resident but non-UK domiciled, purchasing overseas property can offer a number of attractive tax breaks. For income tax and capital gains tax purposes the remittance basis can apply. This means that any rental income obtained from the overseas property will be exempt from UK tax, provided the income is not remitted to the UK.

In addition, when the property is eventually sold, no UK capital gains tax will be payable unless the funds are brought into the country.

The downsides to non-doms achieving these tax benefits are:

£30,000/£50,000 Tax Charge

If you've been UK resident for more than 7 of the last 10 tax years you'll need to pay the £30,000 tax charge for the privilege of using the remittance basis.

This will be treated as a £30,000 tax charge on the overseas rental income and would then allow a proportion of the income to be remitted free of tax in the future. However, unless the rental income was substantial or there was other significant overseas unremitted income, it's unlikely that the remittance basis would be claimed in the first place.

A substantial capital gain though on overseas property could easily make paying the £30,000 tax charge worthwhile.

Once you've been UK resident for 12 years the £50,000 charge kicks in. Even this could be worth paying if the gain retained abroad was substantial.

Overseas Tax Position

The benefit of the remittance basis is for many more apparent than real. Overseas tax is likely to be payable, unless the property is purchased in a tax haven of some kind. Most double tax treaties state that immovable property can be taxed in the country in which it is located (in other words, the overseas jurisdiction) as well as the owner's country of residence. Therefore for a non-UK domiciliary investing in overseas property it is overseas tax that will have the biggest impact.

For example, in Spain sales of property by non-Spanish residents are taxed at 21%.

The gain is calculated as the difference between the sales price and the original purchase price, including any investment made or improvement work carried out. There is also an adjustment to take account of inflation. In addition, the purchaser must retain 3% of the price and pay this as tax on behalf of the non-resident.

The non-UK domiciled UK resident investing in Spain will also need to pay any local taxes relating to the property, as well as other domestic taxes. For example, Spain has reintroduced a wealth tax, which could tax the value of a non-resident's Spanish assets above €700,000.

In France, as a non-resident, the UK resident non-domiciliary pays capital gains tax on the gain arising on the disposal of French property. This is usually deducted from the sale proceeds by the 'Notaire' who pays it over to the local tax authorities.

At present, EU residents pay capital gains tax at the rate of 19%.

It is possible to deduct costs such as original purchase costs (notaire's fee, estate agent's fee) and the cost of renovation work (but not simple redecorating costs), provided that these haven't also been offset against any rental income.

The amount of the taxable gain is then subject to taper relief if it has been owned for more than five years. For each year that the property has been held beyond this initial five-year period, the gain is reduced by 10% (for ten years of ownership, the reduction is thus 50%). Therefore, if a property has been owned for more than 15 years, the relief is 100% and no capital gains tax is payable.

Just as in the UK, there are a number of exclusions and exemptions, and if you are considering purchasing a property in any overseas jurisdiction, it is essential to obtain tax advice from a tax specialist in the country in question.

The only sure-fire way for a non-domiciliary to avoid overseas capital gains tax altogether is to purchase overseas property in a country that:

- Levies no capital gains tax, for example the Isle of Man.

- Levies no taxes at all, for example a tax haven such as Monaco or the Bahamas.

- Has specific exemptions to exclude any gain from a tax charge (for example, Italy or France).

Inheritance Tax

Again, from a UK tax perspective, there would be no UK inheritance tax impact. As a non-UK domiciliary, your taxable estate would include only your UK assets. However, overseas tax would be payable, unless the property was located in a country that did not levy inheritance tax.

Use of Trusts

As a non-UK domiciliary, an offshore trust could be created. For inheritance tax purposes, the trust would not be subject to UK IHT if the assets of the trust were overseas assets.

From an income tax and capital gains tax perspective, the trustees should not be liable to UK income tax on overseas income or UK capital gains tax, if the trust was non-resident.

However another effect of the April 2008 tax changes is that many of the UK anti-avoidance provisions that didn't use to apply to non UK domiciliaries now do apply. These have the effect of attributing and deeming gains of offshore trusts to non UK domiciled trust beneficiaries in various circumstances.

Provided the overseas jurisdiction did not levy capital gains tax, there would also be no overseas tax charge (for example in the Isle of Man).

7.13   THE EFFECT OF UK DOMICILE STATUS ON UK INHERITANCE TAX

If you are a foreign national living and working in the UK you are likely to have a non UK domicile of origin. On the assumption that you have not made the UK your domicile of choice you would therefore be a non UK domiciliary for tax purposes.

You can however be deemed to be a UK domiciliary for inheritance tax purposes only. This would only occur after you have been UK resident for at least 17 tax years.

Assuming you have not been UK resident for the last 17 years you will therefore be non UK domiciled.

If you are non UK domiciled and have a UK domiciled spouse, the usual rules relating to transfers between spouses don't apply.

In particular, spouses who are both UK domiciled can pass assets between themselves without the transfers being taken into account for inheritance tax purposes.

In the case of a transfer from a UK domiciled spouse to a non UK domiciled spouse this exemption is restricted to £55,000. Any amounts above this would usually be treated as potentially exempt transfers (PETs).

As such if the UK domiciled spouse survived for seven years from the date of the transfer it would be excluded from his or her estate for inheritance tax purposes.

If however the UK domiciled spouse was to die within those seven years the amount transferred would be included in the estate. This would be subject to the standard inheritance tax rules and deductions and the nil rate band (currently £325,000) would be available for offset.

It was announced in the March 2012 Budget that the Government is to consider increasing the £55,000 inheritance tax exemption for transfers from a UK domiciled spouse to a non-domiciled spouse, with a view to enacting legislation from April 2013.

Impact of Claim for Arising Basis

After April 2008 you can elect to be taxed on the arising basis for income and capital gains tax purposes.

By claiming the arising basis you will be taxed on your worldwide income and capital gains irrespective of whether they are remitted to the UK or not.

Many non UK domiciliaries will opt for this treatment as their overseas income or gains are not sufficient to cover the annual £30,000 or £50,000 tax charge they would otherwise have to pay.

However the claim to be taxed on the arising basis from April 2008 will only have an effect for income tax and capital gains tax.

For inheritance tax purposes the position would remain as above and any transfers from the domiciled spouse to you would be restricted to £55,000.

How Can the £55,000 Restriction Be Avoided?

This restriction to £55,000 is of concern to many non domiciliaries. It should be noted though that, as above, the nil rate would still be available as well as the usual inheritance tax reliefs and exemptions. In addition if the donor spouse survived for seven years it would in any case be excluded from their estate.

It should also be initially considered whether reliefs such as business property relief (for unquoted shares or business transfers) and the nil rate band would cover any potential liability.

In terms of being eligible for the inter-spouse exemption, another important point is that the £55,000 restriction only applies to transfers from a UK domiciled spouse to a non domiciled spouse.

Any transfers from a non UK domiciled spouse to a UK domiciled spouse would fall within the inter-spouse exemption. Therefore you (if you are a non UK domiciliary) could transfer assets to your spouse with the benefit of the exemption and the transfers would not be taken into account for inheritance tax purposes.

Secondly you could argue that you were a UK domiciliary. If you were electing for the arising basis in any case (and intended to do so) it would not have an impact for UK income or capital gains tax purposes. If you argued that you'd made the UK your domicile of choice you would be a UK domiciliary and the inter-spouse exemption would apply in full for inheritance tax purposes to all transfers between you and your spouse. The downside is that your overseas assets would fall within the scope of UK inheritance tax.

In order to make the UK your domicile you would argue that although you have an overseas domicile of origin you have made the UK your domicile of choice. This would need to be on the basis of making the UK your permanent home, and you intend to remain here indefinitely.

Relinquishing your non UK domicile status though may be a big step and you should always ensure you take detailed advice before taking any action in this area. With a view to making this easier, in the 2012 Budget the Government also announced that it will consider introducing an election for non-UK domiciliaries to be treated as UK domiciliaries for inheritance tax purposes. This change may be enacted in April 2013.

Chapter 8

Working Overseas:
A Powerful Tax Shelter

8.1   INTRODUCTION

If you go abroad under a full-time contract of employment you will usually be regarded as non-resident and not ordinarily resident from the date of departure if:

*   All your work duties are performed overseas, or any duties performed in the UK are incidental to the overseas employment, and

*   Your absence from the UK is for a period which includes a complete tax year, and

*   Visits to the UK do not exceed six months or more in a tax year, or three months or more on average over the period of absence, subject to a maximum of four years.

This status will apply from the day following your departure until the day preceding the day you return. This rule also applies to your spouse if he or she goes abroad with you. Therefore, provided one spouse works overseas and satisfies the above requirements, the accompanying spouse will also be regarded as non-resident and not ordinarily resident from the date of departure.

This means any UK income will be liable to UK income tax, whereas the overseas income will be completely exempt. From a capital gains tax perspective although you're non-UK resident and non-UK ordinarily resident, most overseas employees won't be able to escape UK CGT, as the scope of the CGT rules has been widened. There will be no UK capital gains tax on either UK or overseas assets owned at the date of departure, provided you are non-resident during the tax year of disposal and you remain overseas for a period of five complete tax years.

Note that this five-year rule does not apply to assets purchased after you become non-UK resident – you would be exempt from

UK capital gains tax on these provided you were non-resident during the tax year of disposal.

Example

John is a UK resident and domiciled individual who works for a UK company. He has been offered a 12-month overseas secondment to work full time for the company's Ruritanian subsidiary company. The secondment is to commence on 1st November 2012 and John will return to the UK on 30th October 2013. Any problems?

The key problem here is that while John may satisfy the other requirements relating to working overseas, his absence from the UK does not span a complete tax year. This would therefore result in John being UK resident for the entire tax year and his overseas income being subject to UK income tax.

8.2   TAX-DEDUCTIBLE EXPENSES

Where an employee is resident and ordinarily resident in the UK and performs all work duties abroad, the cost of travelling abroad to take up the employment and returning to the UK on its termination is allowable as a tax deduction.

If travel is only partly for the above purpose, relief is restricted to the relevant part.

Where the overseas duties necessitate the expense of board and lodging for the employee outside the UK and this expense is met by the employer, no tax liability will arise for the employee on the payments made.

Where you have two or more jobs, the duties of one or more of which are performed totally or partly overseas, you are entitled to tax relief for the cost of travelling between the jobs where either or both places are outside the UK.

Where an employee works overseas for a continuous period of 60 days or more, the payment by the employer for a visit by the employee's spouse/children (including a return ticket) will not be taxable.

8.3   TAX-FREE TERMINATION PAYMENTS

A termination payment made to an employee can be partially free of tax provided the employer had no contractual obligation to make the payment. Assuming this is satisfied, Section 401 ITEPA 2003 will usually apply, and the first £30,000 of the termination payment will be tax free.

However where an employee has substantial foreign service it is possible to obtain additional relief and in certain circumstances to totally eliminate any UK income tax charge.

In order to totally shelter the payment from UK tax, the period of employment must include foreign service which includes:

* Three-quarters of the whole period of service.

* Where service has exceeded 10 years, the whole of the last 10 years.

* If more than 20 years' service, half the period plus 10 of the last 20 years.

Where these conditions are not met, the amount exempt after any other deductions (such as the £30,000 exemption) will be in the proportion of foreign service to total service. In other words, a straightforward pro rata of time spent overseas to UK employment.

Example

Johnny commences employment with XYZ Plc in January 2003. He spends two years working at the overseas office in Germany. He is made redundant in January 2012 and is to be offered £100,000 as an ex gratia termination payment.

As Johnny's foreign service does not meet the above criteria, the amount that will be exempt will be two-ninths.

Therefore the taxable amount will be calculated as follows:

Termination payment	*£100,000*
Less S401 exemption	*-£30,000*
	£70,000
Less foreign service relief	
2/9 x £70,000	*-£15,556*
Taxable receipt	*£54,444*

8.4   PROTECTING YOUR PROPERTY INVESTMENTS FROM THE TAXMAN

An individual who works abroad for a number of years may decide to keep a UK residence.

If the property is subsequently sold, will the gain be subject to UK capital gains tax?

Obviously if the individual satisfies the non-residence/ordinary residence criteria at the date of disposal then any gain will be outside the scope of UK capital gains tax.

If the individual is UK resident/ordinarily resident at the date of disposal, it is necessary to look at the application of the Principal Private Residence (PPR) relief, in anticipation of returning to the UK to live in the property.

The PPR relief provides full or partial relief from capital gains tax for an individual who has occupied a property as his main residence at some point during the period of ownership.

A gain on a property will be completely exempt from capital gains tax if an individual has occupied the property as his main residence throughout his entire period of ownership.

Where an individual has occupied a property as a residence for only part of his period of ownership, a proportion of the capital gain resulting on the disposal of the property is tax free. This is calculated on the following basis:

Capital Gain   x   Occupation Period/Ownership Period

In addition to the period that an individual actually occupies a property as his residence, when calculating the period of occupation, there are certain deemed periods of occupation that are allowed to be taken into account.

Most notably, the last 36 months of ownership would always be deemed to be private occupation, irrespective of whether you actually occupied the property during this period. Please note that this relief will only apply where the property has been your main residence at some point during your ownership.

Therefore an individual does not need to reside in a property during the last 36 months of ownership in order to gain full exemption from capital gains tax on a subsequent disposal.

Example

Samantha purchased a property in December 2003 for £50,000. She lived in the property as her main residence until June 2010 when she decided to move in with her boyfriend.

The property was then left empty until June 2012 when she decided to sell it. Any gain on the property when disposed of in June 2012 would be fully exempt from capital gains tax.

She actually lived in the house until June 2010, and the period from June 2010 until June 2012 is covered by the last 36 months 'deemed occupation' rule.

A problem occurs if the 36 months rule does not fully cover the period when the property was not occupied (in other words, the taxable portion). What is the position then?

Fortunately, there is a special provision that relates to individuals working overseas (and in various other circumstances).

Any period during which the owner works full time in an employment wholly outside the UK, provided that both before AND after those periods it was the owner's only or main residence, and assuming he had no other main residence, is deemed private occupation.

Example

Peter purchased a house in 2002 and lived in this as his main residence until 2010. He then travelled abroad until 2012.

On his return he should ensure that he resumes occupation of the property. His period spent overseas would then not restrict the availability of the PPR exemption when he sells the property.

Chapter 9

Making Use of Double Tax Relief

9.1   INTRODUCTION

UK residents have to pay UK tax on income from UK and overseas sources. To prevent overseas income being taxed twice – once abroad and again in the UK – relief is given in one of two ways:

*   By deducting the overseas tax from the UK tax – this is known as credit relief or

*   By charging to UK tax the net amount of overseas income received. In other words, the amount of foreign income after foreign tax has been deducted – this is known as expense relief.

9.2   CREDIT RELIEF

The overseas income is deemed to be the top slice of income for these purposes – in other words, potentially taxed at the higher rates of 40% or 50% (reducing to 45% from April 2013). If there is more than one source of foreign income, double tax relief on each source must be considered separately.

The income with the highest overseas tax is treated as the top slice of overseas income.

Credit relief is given as the lower of:

*   The UK tax on the overseas income
*   The overseas tax

Remember that, as complex as the rules are, the principal objective is to ensure that you do not obtain as a tax credit more than the UK rate of tax.

Therefore, if the overseas tax was charged at 50%, with UK tax being 40%, you would obtain DTR at 40%. Similarly, if the overseas tax was charged at 20%, and UK tax is 40%, you would only obtain DTR at 20%. This is best illustrated with an example.

Example

Doug, a UK resident individual, has the following income in the 2012/13 tax year:

Salary from UK employment	*£45,000*
UK dividends	*£1,875 (Gross)*
Overseas bank interest	*£1,100 (50% foreign tax paid)*

His tax calculation would be:

Salary from UK employment	*£45,000*
Overseas income	*£1,100*
UK dividends	*£1,875*
Less personal allowance	*(£8,105)*
Taxable income	*£39,870*

The income tax levied on this taxable income would be reduced by double taxation relief (DTR).

As the overseas income will be subject to tax at the higher rate (because Doug's salary pushes him into the higher-rate tax band and the overseas income is regarded as the 'top slice' of income) we can calculate that the DTR will be the lower of

- *The UK tax on overseas income (40% x £1,100) = £440*
- *The overseas tax (50% x £1,100) = £550*

Therefore total DTR in this case would be £440, and this would be given as a credit against Doug's tax liability.

It should be noted that if Doug had a tax loss for the period (for example, if he were self employed and had established a trading loss for offset against his other income) then the credit relief described above would be of little use as there would be no tax liability to offset the DTR against. In such a situation, expense relief is most beneficial.

9.3   EXPENSE RELIEF

As stated above, expense relief operates in a totally different way to credit relief. Instead of a credit for overseas tax, the overseas tax is simply deducted from the income before it is subject to UK tax. In other words, it is a deduction from the income rather than the tax on the income.

In most circumstances, credit relief will be far more beneficial but where an individual has no tax charge against which credit relief can operate, expense relief will be better, as it will increase the amount of the loss.

The best way to illustrate this is by means of an example.

Example

Doug's tax position for the next tax year, 2013/14, is as follows:

Overseas income (taxed at 50%)   £1,500
UK trading loss   (£10,000)

No DTR will be given and the trading loss of £8,500 (£10,000 minus £1,500) can be carried forward against future profits of the business.

Expense relief provides a better outcome. It is calculated as the net amount of overseas income, in other words £1,500 less 50% overseas tax = £750.

This increases Doug's trading loss to £9,250 (£10,000 - £750).

Chapter 10

Tax Benefits of Offshore Trusts

10.1 INTRODUCTION

An offshore trust is a legal entity into which you can pass ownership and control of your assets. The assets are then managed by a trustee (such as a trusted firm of accountants or lawyers) in the interests of the beneficiaries (your family, for example). The person who puts the assets into the trust (the settlor) may have a variety of reasons for distancing himself or herself from the ownership of the assets. For example, to remain anonymous for personal or business purposes or to avoid tax.

Offshore trusts are usually set up in tax havens or low tax jurisdictions such as the Channel Islands.

Please note that you should only consider using offshore trusts (and other offshore structures) after receiving advice from a qualified professional who fully understands your personal circumstances.

10.2 HOW OFFSHORE TRUSTS ARE TAXED

From April 6th 2007, a trust would only be non-resident if either all the trustees were non-resident, or if some of the trustees are non-resident and the settlor was non-UK domiciled and non-resident when the trust was set up.

As the trust is non-resident it is not usually subject to capital gains tax in respect of UK or overseas assets (in other words, the same as an individual). Subject to anti-avoidance legislation, offshore trusts are therefore capable of sheltering both UK and foreign capital gains.

Note that this test applies for the purposes of income tax and capital gains tax only – not inheritance tax. In order to be exempt from UK inheritance tax the trust would need to be an 'excluded property settlement' and established by a non domiciled settlor (and consist of overseas assets).

136

As has been mentioned earlier in relation to individuals, non-residents are not subject to UK tax on foreign income and therefore, in the absence of anti-avoidance legislation, offshore trusts can shelter such income. However, trusts are subject to income tax if the source of the income is the UK (just as an individual would be). Different trusts pay tax at different rates, although the type of trust most likely to be used in offshore tax planning would be a discretionary trust.

In 2012/13 these trusts would pay tax at 42.5% on UK dividends, 50% on other income and 28% on capital gains in certain circumstances.

10.3 CAPITAL GAINS TAX CONSEQUENCES

The disposal of assets into a trust is a chargeable disposal for capital gains tax purposes and therefore a capital gain would arise. As the settlor is deemed to be 'connected' with the trust, and proceeds would be deemed to be equivalent to the market value of the assets transferred, it would therefore not be possible to avoid capital gains tax by simply gifting the assets.

The most effective way of establishing a trust from a capital gains tax perspective would be to invest cash and let the trustees use this to invest as they see fit (in accordance with the trust deed). As the asset gifted is cash it falls outside the scope of capital gains tax.

Another possibility would be to settle assets that have a low initial value but which are expected to show significant growth in value. For example, shares in a newly formed company. Any growth in the value of the shares would occur offshore and, subject to the anti-avoidance rules, be outside the scope of UK capital gains tax.

Example

Eric is considering purchasing a share in a small South African mining company for £100,000. He is hoping that the mine will strike gold and the shares will rocket in value. Rather than purchase the shares in his own name, he goes to see his solicitor and forms an offshore trust into which he settles the £100,000. The trust then purchases the shares in the South African company. Any increase in value of the company would be effectively tax free as the trust would be outside the scope of UK capital gains tax. However, as we shall see, matters are not always that simple.

10.4 INHERITANCE TAX CONSEQUENCES

A trust is subject to UK inheritance tax if the settlor was domiciled or deemed to be domiciled in the UK when he set up the trust.

Example

Stefano is of Italian domicile and has moved to Britain to expand his business into the UK. He has substantial assets in Italy and wishes to protect these from inheritance tax. If Stefano sets up an offshore trust, provided he is not UK domiciled at the date of creation or subsequent addition of assets to the trust, the overseas assets will be outside the scope of UK inheritance tax, irrespective of the fact that Stefano may later acquire a UK domicile.

The problem with an offshore discretionary trust is that it can lead to a large inheritance tax cost for a UK domiciled individual (non-UK domiciliaries are considered in detail below).

A transfer of assets to a discretionary trust is called a chargeable lifetime transfer (CLT). This means that a proportion of inheritance tax is paid during the settlor's lifetime.

There are a number of complex rules governing this area. However, in essence the available nil rate band remaining is deducted from the value of the gift (in other words, the assets transferred into the trust) and tax is payable at 20% or 25% depending on whether the trust or the settlor is to pay the tax.

There is also a regime for taxing the assets of the trust. This is necessary, as when you transfer assets into a discretionary trust they are taken out of your estate and are therefore not subject to inheritance tax along with other assets you own.

The 2006 Budget also extended the discretionary trust provisions to most lifetime transfers to other types of trusts (for example accumulation and maintenance trusts established for the education of grandchildren). However, most offshore trusts established would, in any case, usually be discretionary.

The inheritance tax consequences of this discretionary trust treatment are not straightforward and the calculation is pretty complex. What happens is that an effective rate of IHT is calculated based on the initial value of the trust (taking into account previous transfers and all reliefs) based on IHT payable at 6%.

Then when assets are distributed out of the trust, and on every tenth anniversary of the date the trust is set up, inheritance tax is payable on the amount distributed or the trust assets. This ensures that the trust is subject to a form of inheritance tax.

In summary, there are two main circumstances where a discretionary trust is free of inheritance tax:

• Where the trust is within the settlor's nil rate band and remains within the nil rate band for the following 10 anniversaries. The key problem with this trust is that its value is limited to the amount of the nil rate band (currently £325,000).

One possible planning use could be to use the trust as a holding device in which the value of funds initially settled is low and then perhaps distribute the funds before the trust's 10th anniversary. The benefit of this is that for an exit before the first 10-year anniversary, the rate of inheritance tax is based on the value of funds when the trust was created. In this case there would be no inheritance tax exit charge.

• Where the assets transferred into the trust are covered by an inheritance tax exemption such as Business Property Relief (BPR). This relief provides for a full or partial exemption from inheritance tax where 'business assets' are gifted. Typical business assets include assets used in a trade, shares in unquoted trading companies and certain commercial property. There are a number of other conditions that would need to be satisfied to successfully claim Business Property Relief.

10.5 DANGERS FOR UK DOMICILIARIES

There are two principal obstacles that UK domiciliaries have to overcome to shelter their income and gains through an offshore trust:

- Tax anti-avoidance legislation which attributes *income* to the settlor. The income of an offshore trust is assessable as the settlor's if the actual or potential beneficiaries include him, his spouse or minor children or if any of them receives a benefit.

- Anti-avoidance legislation which attributes *gains* to the settlor. The provisions attribute gains to the settlor where any 'defined persons' are actual or potential beneficiaries who receive a benefit from the trust. The term 'defined person' includes the settlor and his spouse, their children, their children's spouses, their grandchildren and their grandchildren's spouses. Clearly this is a particularly wide anti-avoidance provision.

10.6   WHEN AN OFFSHORE TRUST CAN SAVE YOU TAX

There are three main situations where it is still possible for an offshore trust to operate as a tax shelter for a UK domiciled settlor:

1. Where the Settlor is Dead

Clearly the rules attributing income and gains to the settlor cannot apply if he is dead. This could arise if a trust is formed under the terms of a will.

In this case the assets would secure a tax-free uplift in their base cost for capital gains tax purposes (as the assets would pass into the trust at the market value at the date of death).

Of course the assets passing into the trust would be subject to any inheritance tax on death unless the value transferred falls within the nil rate band, or the assets are covered by any other inheritance tax reliefs (such as Business Property Relief).

Example

John's estate consisted of:

House	*£250,000*
Cash	*£50,000*
Shares	*£500,000*

Assuming that the shares were in an unquoted trading company, they would qualify for Business Property Relief (BPR) and the inheritance tax position would be as follows:

House	*£250,000*
Cash	*£50,000*
Nil rate band	*-£300,000*
Shares	*£500,000*
BPR	*-£500,000*

Therefore the inheritance tax charge would be nil.

Any subsequent gain arising on a disposal by John's heirs would be subject to UK capital gains tax (assuming the heirs are UK resident).

By contrast, John could have inserted a provision in his will for the shares to be settled in a non-resident discretionary trust. Inheritance tax would not be an issue, as the shares would qualify for BPR and, although John was a UK domiciliary, the anti-avoidance provisions should not apply as he is dead.

Assuming a subsequent disposal of the shares at a significant gain this would be outside the scope of UK capital gains tax as the gain would now be realised by a non-resident trust.

2. Trusts with All Defined Persons Excluded

Trusts where 'defined persons' are all excluded would not be subject to the anti-avoidance provisions attributing income or gains of the trust to the settlor. However, this is difficult to achieve because, for capital gains tax purposes, defined persons include the settlor, his spouse, children, grandchildren and all their spouses. Therefore, in order to totally exclude all defined persons, the trust would only be able to benefit your friends or remote relations (nephews, nieces etc).

A particular use may be where assets are expected to increase in value rapidly. The initial funds required may be low and an individual could persuade a friend to contribute the initial funds.

Due to the low initial value of the assets, there is unlikely to be any inheritance tax payable on the transfer, and any chargeable gain to date should in any case be minimal.

In this case, the settlor would be your friend and you would be the beneficiary.

The anti-avoidance provisions should not apply provided the settlor (in other words, the friend) does not benefit from the trust and he funds the initial cash required out of his own pocket and not under any agreement, for example in order to receive a future benefit.

The trust would therefore be capable of achieving the capital gains tax and income tax advantages mentioned above including an exemption from CGT on a subsequent disposal, without the gain being apportioned back to the UK resident settlor.

3. Grandchildren's Settlements

You could establish an offshore trust for the benefit of grandchildren and this would still be an effective shelter of foreign income, although not foreign gains. (This arises as the anti-avoidance provisions applying to capital gains tax are much wider than the income tax provisions.) Common assets for the trust to hold would be either shares in a non-resident trading company or a portfolio invested abroad for income.

Example

Peter, a UK resident and domiciled individual, settles cash in an offshore trust for the benefit of his grandchildren who are UK resident. He and his wife are specifically excluded from the class of beneficiaries in the trust deed. The trustees use the cash to purchase shares in an overseas company. Any dividends received by the offshore trust would not be liable to UK income tax. Clearly if a UK trust was used, UK income tax would be fully chargeable on dividends received.

This would then allow a tax-free roll up of funds offshore. If the trust were to pay a distribution to the UK-resident grandchildren, UK tax would be payable, although the grandchildren would always have the option of becoming non-resident themselves and obtaining the cash free of UK tax during a year of non-residency (for example, by taking a 'year out').

142

If the trustees were to sell some of the shares, the gains would be apportioned to Peter as he was the settlor and because the beneficiaries include individuals from an excluded class.

10.7   UK RESIDENT BUT NOT UK DOMICILED

In the absence of a trust, the best strategy for a non-domiciliary is to keep his investments (along with any income/proceeds) outside the UK. In this way any income tax/capital gains tax liability is avoided by claiming the remittance basis, and inheritance tax only applies to his UK assets/estate.

If the non domiciliary has been UK resident for more than seven tax years they may need to take into account the £30,000/£50,000 annual tax charge payable on claiming the remittance basis. If the tax savings from the unremitted overseas income or gains would not cover the tax charge, it would not make sense to claim the remittance basis. If the arising basis was chosen the investments could be kept in the UK as the only tax advantage of overseas investments would be the potential inheritance tax exemption.

If the remittance basis was claimed one of the problems is that the deemed domicile rules may apply for inheritance tax purposes and treat the individual as UK domiciled for inheritance tax purposes. This would have the effect of subjecting his worldwide estate to UK inheritance tax. There is also, of course, the risk that the individual creates sufficient intention to stay in the UK that he obtains a UK domicile.

Use of a trust could help to avoid these risks. If a non-UK domiciliary establishes a trust of which he is a beneficiary, the property in the trust is termed 'excluded property' provided:

* The settlor was not UK domiciled (or deemed domiciled) at the time the trust was established, and

* The trust property is situated outside of the UK.

Example

Terry, a UK resident, but of US domicile, has been resident in the UK for 15 years. He owns substantial assets in both the UK and the US and eventually intends to move back to the US and enjoy his retirement. Once Terry has been resident in the UK for 17 years he will have deemed domicile. This will mean that in the event of his untimely death, the whole of his estate would be taxed in accordance with the UK inheritance tax legislation. If Terry was to transfer his non-UK assets into a trust now (in other words, before he is deemed UK domiciled), the American assets would be excluded property and outside the scope of UK inheritance tax.

Capital Gains Tax

An excluded property settlement also has a number of advantages from a capital gains tax perspective.

Under the current rules, provided the trustees aren't UK resident, the trust is not subject to UK capital gains tax (unless the UK assets of the trust are used in a UK branch/agency trade).

Tax anti-avoidance rules will attribute the gains of the trust to any UK settlor/beneficiary and the trust gains are treated as their individual gains.

Before 6th April 2008 when the beneficiary was non-UK domiciled these rules did not apply and therefore, provided the beneficiary remained non-domiciled, any trust gains were outside the UK capital gains tax net. This still applies in terms of a non UK domiciled settlor.

However in terms of beneficiaries, along with the changes to the remittance basis, they've tightened up on the anti avoidance provisions for non UK domiciliaries.

The broad intention of the changes was to level the playing field between owning personally in your own name and owning via a trust or company. Therefore the effect of the changes is to introduce the remittance basis for any gains of the trust to ensure that only remitted gains are attributed to UK resident beneficiaries (even if non UK domiciled).

The 'settlor charge' that attributes gains of offshore trusts to UK resident settlors will still not apply to non UK domiciliaries (although a settlor could be caught as a beneficiary under the above rules).

Example

Joe a UK resident, but with Greek domicile, settles some assets into an offshore discretionary trust for the benefit of other family members. If the trust later sells the assets at a gain of £1 million there will be no UK capital gains tax charge. The anti-avoidance provisions will not attribute the gain to Joe as he's a UK settlor but non UK domiciled.

The 2008 Budget included provisions to ensure that only gains arising after 5th April 2008 were subject to the new anti avoidance rules for trust beneficiaries. Therefore existing trusts have an option to 'rebase' assets to the value at 5th April 2008 to prevent any gains arising before this date from being apportioned to beneficiaries.

Income Tax

Again the anti-avoidance provisions are amended, the effect of which can be that any UK income of the trust is taxed as the settlor's, whereas foreign income could be subject to the remittance basis and may escape UK income tax, provided the income is kept overseas by the trustees. If the settlor beneficiary subsequently acquires a UK domicile:

- The inheritance tax position of the trust remains the same (in other words, provided the property is situated overseas, then the trust property is outside the scope of UK inheritance tax).
- For capital gains tax, any gains of the trust would become taxed on the settlor as they arise.
- The worldwide income of the trust would be taxed on the settlor on an arising basis.

Example

Eduardo, who was originally born in Latvia, has been UK resident for the last 15 years. He made good use of the benefits of being a non-UK domiciliary as regards offshore trusts and has established such trusts, which now contain significant assets.

He is in the process of disposing of the last of his Latvian assets and is concerned that, given his particular circumstances, he may be classed as having UK domicile.

145

This would be disastrous for Eduardo and income and gains of the trust would be taxable as they arise rather than on the remittance basis (assuming that the remittance basis is claimed).

Sheltering from Overseas Tax

Depending on the overseas country's domestic tax rules, using an overseas trust can help to minimise overseas tax, particularly inheritance tax, and prevent the establishment of an overseas estate.

Example

David, a non-UK domiciliary is considering investing in property in South Africa. If he uses the offshore trust/company structure, the big advantage is that he will not be regarded as owning South African assets. As such he will not be subject to overseas inheritance tax, and may not be subject to the South African estate laws.

10.8   TAX TREATMENT OF DISTRIBUTIONS FROM OFFSHORE TRUSTS TO UK RESIDENTS

Beneficiaries of offshore trusts often want to know how to extract cash from the trust tax efficiently. Broadly speaking there are two options:

- Income distribution
- Capital distribution

Income Distributions

Distributions of trust income to a UK beneficiary are subject to UK income tax.

If the beneficiary is a non UK domiciliary and is subject to the remittance basis they could avoid income tax by retaining the cash overseas. For most non-doms using the remittance basis would mean losing the benefit of UK tax allowances and also raise the spectre of the £30,000/£50,000 remittance basis charge.

It's worth noting that if the beneficiary is also the trust settlor special rules apply to tax the income and gains on the settlor directly.

Capital Distributions

Capital distributions from an offshore trust will be taxed under the anti-avoidance rules. There are two sets of rules that could apply.

Firstly, there's the transfer of asset provisions that can apply to tax capital distributions as income where there is accumulated 'relevant' income in the trust or underlying company.

'Relevant' income for this purpose means income that arises to the offshore trust or company which can be used to provide a benefit for the beneficiary concerned. Income is only taken into account once for this purpose. Therefore rental income, for instance, received by the trust and held in the trust would be treated as relevant income for this purpose.

If there is any relevant income in the trust and a capital distribution is made, the capital distribution could be taxed on the UK resident beneficiary as income to the extent of the relevant income.

This is subject to the motive exemption.

If there is no relevant income in the trust or if the motive exemption applied there would be no tax charge under this provision. However, in this case the beneficiary would be subject to capital gains tax if there are capital gains in the trust.

The capital gains tax charge on the beneficiary effectively looks to tax capital gains that have arisen to the trust (but were exempt because it is non-resident) on the beneficiary.

There would need to be a separate pool to match the gains with capital payments to beneficiaries. The gains are only allocated to capital payments once.

Non-Doms

Non-doms who use the remittance basis can also be taxed on the remittance basis on the distribution from the trust. This means that although the anti-avoidance rules above can apply to tax the distribution to either income tax or CGT, if the cash is retained abroad no UK tax charge may arise.

Why Make an Income Distribution?

Lots of offshore trusts distribute trust income as income distributions. This has some advantages including:

- Withholding tax borne by the trust is set against UK tax charged on the beneficiary

- The income could be paid to beneficiaries with low or no income (eg children)

- UK tax is avoided if the beneficiary is non-resident or non-domiciled and claims the remittance basis (and retains the income abroad).

Complexity of Capital Distributions

Capital distributions can be very complex. It is essential that the trustees provide a full computation of their income and gains for each year. It is necessary to know the total since commencement of the trust, less any previously allocated to income or capital payments.

If there is no relevant income or capital gains in the trust there would be no tax on the receipt, at least at the date of the payment. If relevant income or capital gains arose in the future, a tax charge could well apply in the future.

An option to avoid a future tax charge would be to distribute all of the trust tax efficiently (or resettle after the tax year of the distribution).

Distributions to a Non-Resident or Non-Dom

A good solution is to distribute the trust fund to a non-resident or a non-dom beneficiary. These distributions would not be taxed either for offshore income or capital gains (subject to the non-dom claiming the remittance basis and retaining the receipt abroad if necessary).

If the entire trust fund or an amount equal to the net trust gains was distributed there should be no further UK tax. In the latter case they could then wait a year and distribute the other trust assets to UK beneficiaries free of UK tax.

10.9   UK PROTECTORS AND OFFSHORE TRUSTS

Protectors are often part and parcel of an offshore trust package and they can provide valuable comfort to the trust settlors (ie the person who establishes the trust) that their wishes and the wishes of the beneficiaries are being taken into account.

The Protector can also act as a liaison between the beneficiaries and the trustees to resolve any disputes which may arise from time to time.

Difference Between a Trustee and Protector

The Protector does not have the same powers as the trustee. In particular, the legal ownership of the trust property is held by the trustee who is responsible for the management and control of the trust and its property.

The Protector, however, is not the registered or legal owner of the trust property and would not be involved with the day to day administration of the trust. He will have to fulfil certain duties and responsibilities and will also be given certain powers under the terms of the trust deed.

Usual Powers of the Protector

Any powers that are given to the Protector are provided for in the trust deed. However, typical powers would be to appoint/remove trustees and beneficiaries. They could also be given wider powers to veto investment recommendations or distributions.

UK Tax and Protectors

A key concern for many establishing offshore trusts is to ensure that all of the trustees are non UK resident.

In particular, if there is one UK resident trustee this could make the trust UK resident unless the settlor was also non UK resident and non UK domiciled when the trust is set up.

It would therefore need to be considered whether a UK resident Protector would make an offshore trust become UK resident even if all of the trustees were non-resident.

In practice this is very unlikely. It would need to be considered whether the Protector could be classed as a trustee for tax purposes. Given that the trust property is not vested in him and provided he does not have power to actually initiate action (only the power to veto proposals put forward by the actual trustees), the Protector should not be classed as a trustee.

To support this, however, any settlor should ensure that the actual trustees have a free rein over how to invest income and capital and also how to distribute income. The role of the Protector should therefore be to veto appointments or to veto large capital distributions.

10.10 WHERE DO YOU SET UP A TRUST AND HOW MUCH DOES IT COST?

There are numerous countries offering an attractive regime for setting up offshore trusts. A trust may be set up or administered anywhere in the world. However, it's essential the jurisdiction in which the trust is established recognises the legal concept of the trust.

The countries listed below all recognise the use of trusts.

The four main reasons for setting up a trust are to:

- Protect your assets from creditors etc
- Maintain confidentiality
- Avoid financial reporting requirements
- Pay less tax

The countries listed below are all recognised as good places to locate an offshore trust. This list is by no means exhaustive and, depending on how the trust will be used and the location of the beneficiaries and the settlor, other countries such as Mauritius and Belize could also be considered.

When choosing where to set up your trust, other significant non-tax considerations could be paramount including the:

- Language used in the jurisdiction.
- Time difference between you and the trust jurisdiction.
- Political and financial stability of the country.
- Geographic proximity – in case you need to travel there.
- Fees associated with setting up and maintaining the trust.

For example, an individual looking at significant trade with China could consider a trust in Mauritius as opposed to St Kitts, due to the close relationship Mauritius has with China.

However, the top locations where a trust can be established at an affordable price are as follows:

- Jersey
- Liechtenstein
- The Cayman Islands
- St Kitts Nevis
- Panama
- Gibraltar
- Isle of Man
- Bermuda
- Bahamas
- Austria
- New Zealand

Obviously financial costs are incurred in setting up and running an offshore trust. It is likely to cost from £1,000-plus for the initial set up and further charges will be incurred for ongoing compliance work and if you require professional advisers to act as trustees.

Please note that, while there are many reputable firms offering offshore tax planning services, there are also many fly-by-night operators providing advice of dubious quality that may land you in considerable trouble with the UK taxman.

It should also be noted that the settlor and beneficiaries of an offshore trust must disclose all relevant information on their tax returns. In addition, when the trust is established the person making the settlement MUST submit a return to Revenue and Customs within three months. Similar provisions also apply to trusts established by non UK residents who subsequently become UK resident.

10.11 USING TRUSTS FOR ASSET PROTECTION

Offshore trusts are popular, not just as tax-saving devices, but also for their perceived *asset protection* benefits.

Many wealthy individuals fear being sued and losing a significant chunk of their wealth. If your assets are visible or easily reached, you are pretty much a sitting duck these days.

Because of this danger many wealthy individuals set up offshore structures to hide their assets or make them difficult to plunder.

A wide variety of people engage in asset protection planning but it's particularly popular with those working in professions where there is a higher risk of litigation:

- Doctors
- Lawyers
- Accountants
- Builders
- Consultants
- Financial advisers

152

Asset protection planning is also popular with those who want to safeguard their money from ex-spouses and other family members, disgruntled employees and business partners.

The bottom line is this: those with deep pockets are perceived as easy prey nowadays. Asset-protection planning acts like a castle moat, protecting your hard-earned wealth from the outside world.

Asset protection measures can be split into three main categories:

Insurance

Pretty obvious in itself, but having good insurance can save a lot of worry. In fact, most professionals or traders are required to have indemnity insurance to cover them against providing negligent advice or faulty goods and services. Although insurance provides a good 'base' level of protection it's unlikely that any policy will cover the full range of potential claims and other more comprehensive asset protection tools are often needed.

Limiting Your Liability

Another way to protect your assets is to set up a company. A company has a separate legal identity, which means in principle any creditors would have to target the company's assets, rather than your own. And if the company doesn't have any assets then the claim will amount to nothing.

However, the courts can and do 'pierce the corporate veil' in certain circumstances. This means they will ignore the limited liability protection provided by the company and instead seek to recover the personal assets of the shareholders or directors.

This is something you would have to discuss with your solicitor, however there are a number of situations where limited liability protection does not work. For example, the Insolvency Act contains special provisions which cover fraudulent trading or wrongful trading.

Essentially, if you carry on trading and incurring liabilities when you know or have reason to believe the company can't pay its debts, the creditors can target your personal assets.

Other situations where the veil can be pierced are:

- Where the use of a company is a sham and it is used for fraudulent purposes.

- Where a 'special relationship' existed between a director of the company and the customer so that the customer relied on a personal assumption of responsibility by the director.

Using a company may not provide any additional protection against such personal claims. However, it could be used to reduce the risk of general business claims.

There are several types of entity that can be used for limited liability protection, including a limited company and a limited liability partnership.

An alternative (especially when combined with the wealth segregation activities discussed below) is to consider using an offshore entity such as a limited liability company (LLC). An LLC has fewer requirements (compulsory annual meetings, directors etc). However, given it is overseas, it would cost much more to set up than a UK company (which can be set up for around £100). We look at the different types of entity in the next chapter.

Ring-Fencing Your Assets

Another option is to look at separating your wealth from your estate. In effect, this means putting it outside the reach of any creditors.

The simplest way to protect an asset is by ensuring that you don't own it any more – by giving it away, for example. However, if this is a sham arrangement, and you still have control over the asset or have use of it (for example, if you occupy a property that you have given away) a court is likely to rule that you have retained the 'beneficial interest' and the asset will be classed as part of your estate.

Using a company is also a way of segregating assets, as by transferring to a company, you are also divesting yourself of ownership. As seen above, the courts can and do ignore the company in certain circumstances. This is why many individuals looking to exclude some of their wealth from their estates use offshore arrangements in countries that have strict privacy laws.

If you set up an offshore company to hold your assets you should try and avoid becoming a shareholder in the company. If you are a shareholder a court is likely to class the value of the shares/company assets as part of your estate.

Note that this is different from simply keeping quiet about the existence of the company. If you choose correctly you can ensure that shareholder details aren't named on any share register, and if they are, it's only the legal owner that is named. You could then use nominees to hold the legal title to the shares, keeping your name off the documents.

Many people do this and are successful on the basis that any creditors would need to find the assets before they can have a slice of them. One point that is worth noting here is that if the segregated assets were to generate any income, this would need to be disclosed on your UK tax return if you are UK resident and domiciled (this would then make it practically impossible to deny the existence of the offshore assets).

That is why, in terms of asset protection, the use of a trust and company is more common than an offshore company on its own.

In a trust arrangement, the settlor gives control of his assets to trustees, who manage and control the trust assets for the beneficiaries (who can include the settlor). Although the settlor will usually provide a letter of wishes, indicating how he would like the trust to operate and the kind of distributions that should be made, it is the trustees that have legal control over the assets.

Trusts could traditionally be used to 'break the link' between an individual and his assets and, although this is now less the case, they can still be effective for this purpose.

The courts take a practical approach to the matter and if you set up a trust, make yourself one of the beneficiaries and receive significant distributions on a regular basis, don't be surprised if a court classes the assets as yours.

This isn't to say that it's not worthwhile using the trust as the offshore nature could make it more difficult to enforce.

However, to be on the safe side, you would be better off if you weren't a beneficiary and received only a limited amount of income from the trust.

Similarly, ensuring that the trustees do not automatically agree to all your requests would also assist in preventing the assets being classed as yours. Basically you want to avoid any argument that the trustees are just 'rubber stamping' any request or direction you give them.

Protecting Assets on Divorce

Many high net worth individuals realise that nowadays a marriage breakdown could pose a massive threat to their wealth. As a result they use offshore structures to protect their assets.

By using a trust spouses facing divorce can simply argue that they are merely discretionary beneficiaries of the trust and that the trust assets should not be treated as their own.

The courts don't always accept this and have the power to go after trust assets when they are made in contemplation of marriage or during the marriage. The terms are widely interpreted and include both UK and offshore trusts.

Even if a trust is not regarded as being made in contemplation of marriage, a court will usually take into account the history of any receipts from the trusts. If there has been a regular income stream, a court would usually take the view that the income would continue (even if it stops at the time of the divorce).

Courts also have wide powers to order disclosure of information relating to trusts as trustees can be asked to be joined as parties to legal proceedings. The main purpose of this would be to get information about the trust from the trustees. This is why *offshore* trusts are popular, as enforcing decisions against offshore trustees is usually more difficult.

Instead, if there are sufficient other assets available, the court may prefer to order a transfer of those assets given that it is much simpler and more cost effective than chasing after assets in an offshore trust. Even so, the value of the offshore trust could be taken into account.

Offshore trusts can be useful vehicles but it is all too easy to think that they can always protect assets on divorce. As shown above, even if your spouse is not a beneficiary a court may well be able to amend a trust to effectively grant them some of the trust assets.

If you are considering using an offshore trust you should, where possible, ensure that there is no expectation of a receipt from the trust. Also, be warned that, if you're thinking of setting up a trust to transfer assets into in case you suffer a marriage breakdown, a court would not look favourably on the arrangement.

In terms of greater security, a person at risk of divorce should, wherever possible, not be a beneficiary of the trust – the spouse should also not be a beneficiary.

This will prevent the trust assets being treated as part of their assets. In addition, it would also make actually getting hold of trust documents more difficult (as only beneficiaries and trustees would usually have a right to see trust documents).

Similar considerations also apply to other asset protection strategies, for example protecting against potential creditors.

Rather than use an offshore entity, many individuals use an offshore bank account to hold their cash. There is no real segregation of wealth here as the cash still plainly belongs to you. This is therefore purely a case of 'hiding' the cash and hoping no one finds out about it. Given that banking secrecy laws in offshore jurisdictions are usually very strict, unless criminal activity or money laundering is suspected, it's unlikely that your details will be made available to a third party in the absence of an exchange of information treaty.

You would need to ensure that any income generated from the offshore account is declared on your tax return. If you don't, you then need to consider the impact of the EU Savings Tax Directive in terms of which the UK tax authorities would be informed of the income, or tax will be withheld from any interest paid.

You should also note that Revenue and Customs is clamping down on people who aren't declaring interest earned from overseas bank accounts and are obtaining information on UK-resident offshore account holders direct from banks. It goes without saying that hiding income from the taxman is not a very clever offshore strategy and you should always disclose when you have to.

The recent G20 clampdown on tax evasion will also lead to more countries signing international exchange of information agreements for tax purposes. These treaties will ensure that information on overseas assets, income and gains can be passed to your home country's tax authorities much more readily.

Asset protection for UK residents is a complex area and the best course of action is to take advice from a lawyer with experience in this area.

10.12 KEEPING A LOW PROFILE

An issue that is related to asset protection is the desire to keep your activities private and avoid intrusion into your affairs.

It's for this reason you need to be mindful as to how your actions are monitored by the authorities.

A good example relates to a colleague of mine. He is a non-UK resident (living in Gibraltar) and has most of his cash and investments outside the UK. However, as he buys a lot of goods from auction websites in the UK, he established a UK bank account to obtain a UK debit card.

However, he was finding purchases of airline tickets and other goods increasingly difficult using a non-UK shipping address. He decided, therefore, to use a UK friend's house as the registered and shipping address.

After he transferred a couple of thousand pounds into the account from overseas he received a letter from the HMRC Compliance Division. The authorities were concerned about the unmatched nature of the account. All information is cross checked these days and when you have cash coming in from overseas to a UK individual, the authorities make sure it ties in with their records.

Of course there was nothing sinister about my colleague's arrangement but the worrying aspect for most people is having to explain to Big Brother how you choose to structure your financial affairs.

There are a number of transactions that can 'red flag' you to the authorities. Some of the more common activities are:

Anything Unusual

In short, anything unusual can set the alarm bells ringing, such as large or frequent transactions from overseas. The UK authorities are pretty paranoid about the 'offshore angle' at the moment, so any unusually large or frequent transfers from overseas will be initially viewed with an element of suspicion.

We're not even talking about massive sums of money. Banks are required to report irregular account activity, so if you normally tick along with an account balance of £1,000 and suddenly £10,000 is transferred into your account from overseas, you may find that you need to explain where the funds came from.

As well as the size of transactions there is also the number of transactions. If you normally use your account for just receiving salary and paying a few direct debits but then suddenly start having lots of Paypal transfers from your Ebay dealings, don't be surprised if you later receive a letter from the UK taxman if you have not been declaring any trading income.

Unmatched Information

If you set up a network of offshore companies, offshore bank accounts and trusts, you need to be careful that the declared signatories, including trustees and directors, all have verifiable addresses. If you use an address that is not registered to you, or rather is registered to someone else, the authorities may pick up on this, particularly if there are also transfers of funds from overseas.

Transferring Assets Overseas

The UK taxman doesn't like assets going outside the UK tax net, so one area the Government agencies keep a close eye on is overseas asset transfers. Pretty obvious really but if you're looking to fund an offshore company, simply transferring the cash from your UK bank account may not be advisable if you're wanting to keep your affairs private. This kind of paper trail will undoubtedly result in the UK authorities knowing about your offshore account.

Offshore Companies

Using an offshore company is a perfectly legitimate commercial and tax-planning strategy. However, as with most strategies, you need to use these with your eyes wide open.

What most of the various offshore incorporation agents (people that set up offshore companies) fail to tell you is that if you use a company established in certain tax havens, this in itself could make the UK authorities take a closer look at your affairs.

Actually deciding which jurisdictions could red flag your activities is difficult, although countries such as Colombia, Ecuador, Russia, Latvia, Thailand, Nigeria, the Cayman Islands, Liechtenstein and Pakistan could be considered higher risk than other jurisdictions.

It's for this reason that the nominee structure has grown in popularity. Essentially, this involves using a company formed in a respected jurisdiction to be the commercial 'face' of the group's activities. The tax haven company would then be a holding company and funds would be channelled to the tax haven. The UK is one of the most popular destinations for nominee companies, given its sound economy, strong international links, low corporate taxation and good double tax treaty network.

The nominee structure works by ensuring that any invoicing comes from the nominee company. A UK customer, for example, may be happier receiving an invoice from a UK company than an overseas company. The UK company would receive the cash and then, as per the nominee agreement, the majority of the funds would be transferred to the overseas company.

It would be important for the UK nominee to retain some income to ensure that this overall structure is viewed as an above-board commercial agreement and usually the nominee would receive an agent's fee calculated on an arm's length basis.

Chapter 11

Tax Benefits of Offshore Companies

11.1 INTRODUCTION

A UK resident company is subject to UK corporation tax on its worldwide income and gains. By contrast a non-UK resident company is only subject to corporation tax on its UK income.

At first glance, therefore, it would seem that an offshore company is an effective way of sheltering income and capital gains from the taxman, as all foreign income and gains accruing to the company should be free of UK tax.

In fact using a *directly owned* offshore company is not a straightforward option to avoid UK taxes. One of the reasons for this is the issue of 'deemed' company residence. A company is regarded as a UK resident if:

- It is a UK incorporated company, or
- Its *central management and control* is in the UK.

Various legal cases have indicated that it is the function of the board of directors to run the company and therefore Revenue and Customs would initially be concerned with where the board of directors meet, when they meet, and whether they actually exercise control over the company and make management decisions.

So if a board of directors meet overseas and review management decisions and strategies this should constitute overseas central management and control.

However, where there is a controlling shareholder in the UK there is a risk that the directors will not correctly exercise their authority over the company with the result that HMRC may argue that the company is run by the controlling shareholder in the UK. In these circumstances the company would be classed as UK resident and subject to UK corporation tax.

11.2 HOW THE TAXMAN SPOTS PHONY OFFSHORE MANAGEMENT

HMRC has stated that it will look at offshore companies to identify if there has been an attempt to create simply the appearance of central management and control in a place.

Therefore, care is needed to ensure that any overseas directors are actually running the company.

In order to pass the central management and control test the majority of the directors should be non-UK resident, and the non-UK resident directors should actively participate in making board decisions.

This therefore means that key business decisions should be taken at overseas board meetings. A UK resident shareholder may therefore establish a non-resident company but it is essential to ensure that the running of the business is left to the non-resident directors.

The central management and control test was looked at by the High court and the Court of Appeal in the 2005 case *Wood v Holden*. The taxpayer in this case successfully argued that the central management and control of an offshore company was overseas.

The facts were complex but essentially a Dutch subsidiary was incorporated which was part of a tax planning scheme. It acquired some shares in a UK company and HMRC felt that, as there was no real business being carried on overseas, the Dutch company should be taxed as a UK resident company.

The appeal commissioners sided with HMRC and took the view that " ... the company resides for purposes of income tax where its real business is carried on where the central control and management actually abides...".

However, both the High Court and the Court of Appeal decided this was wrong. They said that the directors who were non-resident were not sidestepped or bypassed and there was no evidence that UK parties dictated to them. The overseas directors actually executed the board meetings and resolutions.

162

Therefore in the absence of any evidence showing them deferring to other parties, they and the company were non-resident.

This case reinforced the fact that it is essential that overseas directors actually consider the board resolutions and other transactions in order to evidence the fact that they are not under the control of another person. Note that an overseas shareholder having influence over the directors is fine, but there is a problem when the directors simply accept everything the shareholder says and carry out his wishes without any consideration.

11.3   ROLE OF A MANAGING DIRECTOR

If there is a managing director who has exclusive power to run the company, there's a good case for arguing that this person has 'central management and control'.

If you want to use this to argue that one overseas director actually exercises central management and control, it would be advisable to also have this laid out in the company's Articles of Association.

11.4   RECENT CASE ON COMPANY RESIDENCE

One of the latest cases to be considered in relation to the residence of an offshore company was *Laerstate BV v Commissioners*.

This case covers a lot of the issues which we have covered above and provides a useful summary of the key points.

The company in question was incorporated in the Netherlands on 1 August 1988 as a wholly owned subsidiary of another Dutch company. Its sole director on incorporation was an individual ('T').

In December 1992 'B' acquired the entire shareholding in the company and was appointed as a director until he resigned on 30 August 1996. Note that for Dutch tax purposes the company was resident in the Netherlands as it was incorporated there.

The company then purchased an investment in December 1992. In October 1996 the investment was sold at a substantial capital gain. B was UK resident as of 1993.

HMRC subjected the company to corporation tax on the gain on the basis it was resident in the UK for tax purposes at the time the gain arose. The company argued it was not UK resident as it was controlled from overseas. The Tax Tribunal held that it was UK resident.

Remember in this case the shareholder was UK resident and also a director of the company for part of the period of ownership. After he resigned his directorship, 'T' (non-resident) was the director.

As we've stated above the courts look at the top level strategic management of the company and won't be fooled by attempts to have nominees exercising 'fake' control from overseas.

It was no surprise then that the Tribunal found that the company was UK resident, as it was controlled and managed from the UK.

The Tax Tribunal specifically said:

"...it was not disputed that for tax purposes a company resided where the central management and control (CMC) 'abides'.

That was a test that did not confine itself to a consideration of particular actions of the company, such as the signing of documents or the making of certain board resolutions outside the UK if a more general overview of the course of business and trading demonstrated that central management and control 'abides' in the UK.

There was no assumption that central management and control was found where the directors met. It was entirely a question of fact where it was found. Where a company was managed by its directors in board meetings it would normally be where the board meetings were held. But if the management was carried out outside board meetings one had to ask who was managing the company by making high level decisions and where, even where that was contrary to the company's constitution.

There was nothing to prevent a majority shareholder, whether a parent company or an individual majority shareholder, indicating how the directors of the company should act. If the directors considered those wishes and acted on them it was still their decision. The borderline was between the directors making the decision and not making any decision at all.

The mere fact that B was resident in the UK during the relevant period did not of itself mean that the company was resident in the UK. The question was whether he was exercising central management and control in the UK, as he had authority as a director of the company to do. It could not be said that, on the facts in this case, all acts of central management and control of the company took place outside the UK.

B's activities as a director of the company in the UK went much further than ministerial matters or matters of good housekeeping. His activities in the UK were certainly concerned with policy, strategic and management matters, and included decision-making in relation to the company business in that period.

Accordingly, in the period to 30 August 1996, when B resigned as a director, central management and control of the company was exercised in the UK.

In relation to the time after B ceased to be a director, only T could sign for the company in a way that would bind a third party. The issue was whether T acted on B's instructions without considering the merits of them, or whether he considered B's wishes and made the decision himself while in possession of the minimum information necessary for anyone to be able to decide whether or not to follow them.

On the facts found, it could not be said that T made any of those decisions. The decisions were those of B; T signed the necessary documents but no change could be detected in the way the company was managed before and after B ceased to be a director of the company (or before he became a director).

B predominantly made those decisions in the UK and so the company was resident in the UK during the time after B ceased to be a director on 30 August 1996 until at least 31 December 1996."

Therefore this case provides a good indication as to how the Tribunal looks to identify where the 'real' control as opposed to 'apparent' control is exercised from.

It also reinforces the importance of the position of the directors in terms of identifying the central management and control.

It's not just a case of looking at where the shareholders of a company meet. Instead you look to see where the 'controlling mind' of the company's business is to be found.

You would therefore look at the constitution of the company to see who has the power to manage the company's business. Usually this will be the directors.

As such, provided the directors have not been usurped from their position of control, the case law tends to show that the place of residence is the place where the board meets.

Because establishing where the management and control is carried out can be difficult to ascertain, HMRC published some draft guidance on this matter in 2010.

HMRC has specifically stated that it is not the number of UK directors meetings versus the number of overseas meetings that is important. Instead, what is important is what activities are actually carried out at the board meetings.

HMRC also confirmed that the location of a director's tax residence doesn't impact on the residence of the company. Instead it is the location where the management and control are carried out that is important (which is not necessarily the same as the country of tax residence of the director).

How to Establish an Offshore Company as Non-Resident

Clearly you should ensure that detailed professional advice is taken based on your specific facts. As a general rule you should ensure there is an active board which meets and takes decisions.

Some of the key points to bear in mind include:

- Hold at least six board meetings a year (Although three or four should be acceptable).

- Keep full minutes which show the directors exercising central management and control.

- Hold meetings in a fixed place (at least usually).

- Do not hold any board meetings in the UK. In addition you should ensure there is not a quorum of directors resident in the UK (to avoid accidental UK meetings).

- Do not allow directors to participate in directors' meetings by telephone/video conferencing or by using e-mail from within the UK. In addition, where directors' resolutions are passed in writing, don't sign them in the UK.

- If the board wants things done in the UK it needs to delegate the activities to be performed to people in the UK and then supervise what they do at the regular (overseas) board meetings.

11.5   APPORTIONMENT OF CAPITAL GAINS

UK tax anti-avoidance provisions require the gains of a non-resident 'close' company to be apportioned amongst the member shareholders. Capital gains tax is charged on those who are resident and domiciled in the UK.

Before 6th April 2008 these apportionment rules did not apply to non UK domiciliaries. However, the changes to the remittance basis from April 2008 means that if a shareholder is UK resident but non UK domiciled, they will be subject to the remittance basis on any gains realised by the offshore company. As such they can avoid having gains attributed to them under this section by retaining the proceeds overseas.

The definition of a close company can be complex, however in simple terms it applies to a company that is controlled by its directors or five or fewer shareholders.

Example

Jack and Jill are the sole shareholders of JackJill Ltd, a company registered in the Cayman Islands. They hold 50% of the shares each and are both UK resident and domiciled. Assuming they allow non-resident directors to run the company and can satisfactorily show that the company is not centrally managed and controlled from the UK, then the attribution of gains legislation would mean that any gains of the offshore company would be attributed to Jack and Jill (50% each).

However, if Jack was non-UK domiciled and subject to the remittance basis the gains could only be attributed to him to extent he actually brought the gains into the UK.

11.6   BENEFITS IN KIND

If the taxman is able to assert that the company is being managed by the shareholder or that the directors of the company are accustomed to act on his directions, he will be classed as a shadow director and income tax will be payable on any benefit in kind received by him or his family. One of the key benefits in kind that may apply is the accommodation charge. This levies a charge on an employee where he or she is provided with accommodation by an employer.

However, in the 2007 Budget a change was announced to the tax treatment of overseas property companies. The effect is to remove the benefit-in-kind tax charge for investors who buy overseas holiday homes using a company (in many countries investors are forced to buy property through a company).

There are certain conditions that have to be satisfied (for example, the company must own no other assets) but this change removes one of the main drawbacks of using a company to invest in overseas property. However, it doesn't alter the fact that the investor will still have to pay corporation tax instead of income tax or capital gains tax, which may result in a higher tax bill in many circumstances.

11.7   USING A NON-RESIDENT TRUST AND COMPANY

For the reasons stated above, offshore companies that are directly owned by UK residents are not actually that common in practice. Instead, offshore companies *owned by offshore trusts* are used more frequently. Such arrangements are often popular from a non-tax angle due to the practical advantages of owning the trust investments through one or more wholly owned offshore companies. This gives the trustees the benefit of limited liability.

The residence of the company is not a key issue in these circumstances as the only persons legally entitled to exercise control of the company are the non-resident trustees.

However, following on from the *Wood v Holden* case, care would need to be taken to ensure that the company really is run by either the trustees or directors. If they were to stand aside and let a settlor/beneficiary give all the instructions, it could be contended that the company residence is the same as that of the settlor or beneficiary.

Provided the beneficiaries were non-resident, they would suffer no UK taxation charge on distributions from the trust, and the company/trust would also suffer no UK tax charge if the assets held were overseas assets. If the beneficiary is a UK resident, the main problem would be the UK anti-avoidance legislation. There are limited ways of escaping this, and if one of the exemptions applied (for example, the motive test), this could be claimed on the tax return.

The motive test is an important aspect of one of the key anti-avoidance rules that attributes the income of offshore trusts and companies to UK resident individuals. The anti-avoidance provisions will not apply if the transfer overseas was not made for the purpose of avoiding tax or if there was a real commercial reason for transferring assets to an overseas company or trust.

Therefore for an individual to take advantage of this rule, and claim that income from an offshore company or trust should not be attributed to them, they would need to show that there was no tax avoidance motive in the transfer of any asset overseas and essentially that the companies were located overseas for sound commercial reasons. This can be a difficult provision to satisfy.

In order to be non-resident for income tax and capital gains tax purposes under the current rules the trustees would all need to be non-resident if the settlor was UK resident.

Example

Peter, a UK resident and domiciled individual wishes to purchase a business and property in Ibiza. One option would be to establish a trust, and transfer funds to the trustees. They would then either purchase the property directly, or via a wholly owned company.

The transfer of funds from Peter would, however, be a problem from an inheritance tax perspective. As Peter is UK domiciled, the settlement is an immediately chargeable transfer, taxable at 20% for amounts above £325,000 (this assumes that he has made no previous gifts). However, the advantage of using a discretionary trust route is that the property would then be excluded from his estate for inheritance tax purposes. The drawback is that the trust would be subject to a separate regime of UK taxation. For inheritance tax purposes, the trust is subject to UK inheritance tax if Peter was domiciled in the UK when the transfer was made. This would undoubtedly be the case.

In these circumstances one option to exempt the trust from UK inheritance tax would be for the transfer to the trust to be of 'relevant business property'. The transfer to the trust would then be exempt from UK inheritance tax, and the trust itself would not suffer an ongoing inheritance tax charge, as business property relief (BPR) would exclude the property from the inheritance tax charge.

Relevant business property includes a sole trader business, assets used in a partnership and shares in unquoted trading companies. Therefore in this case it would be far better for Peter to purchase the business and property directly and subsequently transfer this to the trust/company.

Provided any transfer was made shortly afterwards, there would be unlikely to be a capital gains tax charge as any increase in value would be minimal.

The trust would then be exempt from UK inheritance tax as the assets transferred would qualify for Business Property Relief.

11.8   USING AN OFFSHORE COMPANY AND TRUST: NON-UK DOMICILIARIES

Many non-UK domiciliaries choose to use this structure to minimise their UK tax liabilities.

Example

Paul is a non-UK domiciliary and wishes to purchase a property in the Isle of Man (IOM). He decides to use an offshore company to own the property with 100% of the shares in the company owned by a non-resident IOM trust. The tax implications are as follows:

Capital Gains Tax

As non-residents the trust and company will not be subject to UK capital gains tax. Provided the beneficiaries are non-UK domiciled, any distribution to the beneficiary should be taxed on the remittance basis (provided they are subject to the remittance basis on their income and gains).

Income Tax

Any income distributions would be taxed on the remittance basis (provided this is claimed). There are anti-avoidance provisions in place so that income earned by the trust is not subject to UK income tax on beneficiaries, unless it is remitted to the UK (again provided the remittance basis is claimed).

Inheritance Tax

The Isle of Man trust is only subject to UK inheritance tax on UK assets, as it was established by a non-UK domiciled individual. By using the offshore company to hold any UK property, there will be no UK inheritance tax on the property, as the trust will hold shares in an IOM company, which are treated as non-UK assets for inheritance tax purposes.

11.9   HOW TO USE YOUR SPOUSE'S OFFSHORE STATUS

Even though you may not be non-resident or non-domiciled, this doesn't necessarily prevent you from taking advantage of certain offshore tax planning opportunities. You may be able to reap rewards if you're lucky enough to have a spouse with some type of 'offshore' status.

The most famous example of this is BHS boss Philip Green. In the past he has routed hundreds of millions of pounds in dividends through his wife. Thanks to her non-UK resident status, these amounts have been completely tax free.

You too could use similar techniques to reduce your UK tax bill if you have a spouse who is either non-resident or non-domiciled.

If your spouse is non-domiciled, chances are he or she will either have been born overseas to foreign parents or, if born in the UK, the parents will be foreign and your spouse will have demonstrated substantial links with the home country (for example, by owning property and having close family ties etc). Furthermore, your spouse will make it clear that he or she does not intend to remain in the UK permanently.

Ideally, your spouse will also not have been UK resident for the last 17 years. In these circumstances he or she will be deemed UK domiciled for inheritance tax purposes. Despite this, there are still lots of tax benefits that can be obtained thanks to being non-UK domiciled, especially if you've not been UK resident for more than 7 of the last 10 tax years.

If your spouse is non-UK resident a significant proportion of the year will have to be spent overseas. There would also have to be no ongoing connection with the UK and the UK should not be 'home' in the ordinary sense of the word.

If your spouse wanted more ties with the UK (for example, by sharing a home here with you for up to 90 days per tax year) he or she should ideally be located in a country which has a tax treaty with the UK. Treaty residence overseas would then be obtained. This would rule out many tax havens which do not have tax treaties with the UK. A low-tax haven such as Cyprus could, however, be considered.

The Benefits of a Non-UK Domiciled Spouse

If you are UK resident and domiciled and your spouse is UK resident but non-domiciled, this opens up some interesting tax planning opportunities.

Many people want to use an offshore company to hold UK or overseas assets. As we've seen, for a UK resident domiciliary many of the advantages of using offshore companies are eliminated by anti-avoidance legislation. If, however, your spouse is non-UK domiciled that person can be used to hold assets or to use offshore companies and trusts in a tax effective manner provided they are subject to the remittance basis.

Some of the key opportunities could include:

- Establishing an offshore company to hold UK assets, in particular property that is not occupied by any directors or shareholders. The main benefit would be to take the assets outside the scope of UK inheritance tax (IHT). Non-UK domiciliaries only pay IHT on their UK assets. But if a UK property is owned by an offshore company, the property is no longer regarded as a UK asset. You would need to be careful to ensure that the company is controlled overseas and that no property owned by the company was occupied by UK resident directors or shareholders (otherwise a UK income tax charge could arise).

- Another benefit is that it's much easier for a non-UK domiciliary to use an offshore company to avoid UK capital gains tax. For UK resident domiciliaries there are strict anti-avoidance rules that class gains that arise to many offshore companies as being those of UK resident shareholders.

  However, if you arrange for a non-domiciled spouse to own the shares, the company can sell assets and realize gains without tax being paid personally by the shareholder provided the proceeds aren't brought into the UK. Again this assumes that the spouse has the benefit of the remittance basis. If not they will be taxed the same as you, a UK domiciliary.

- Holding overseas assets. If you plan to buy overseas assets it makes sense to hold these via your non-domiciled spouse. Not only would these assets then be outside the scope of UK inheritance tax but in addition the remittance basis could apply to overseas income and gains. This means that your spouse (in reality, you as a couple) would only be taxed on any overseas income or gains brought into the UK. This means you could buy or sell shares or property and reinvest the proceeds overseas without paying a penny in tax.

- Establishing an overseas trading company. If you want to establish a company to trade overseas, provided the company can be established as controlled from overseas (for example, using overseas directors), having your spouse as the shareholder means that dividends could be received free of UK income tax, provided the cash is retained overseas.

- Establishing an offshore trust. As we've seen, this is much easier if the settlor (the person who creates the trust) is a non-UK domiciliary.

As from 6th April 2008 though for a non UK domiciled spouse to utilise most of these tax advantages they would need to claim the remittance basis of tax as opposed to the arising basis of tax.

This would then mean that you would need to consider the impact of the loss of allowances for your spouse (personal allowance and the capital gains tax annual exemption) as well as the £30,000 annual tax charge if they've been UK resident for more than seven of the last ten tax years (rising to £50,000 once they've been UK resident for more than 12 years).

Remember for inheritance tax purposes you can also be deemed UK domiciled if you've been UK resident for the previous 17 years, and also for three years after you actually lose your UK domicile. So you have to be careful to ensure that your spouse, although born and domiciled overseas, is also not UK resident for 17 of the previous 20 years.

Limited Inter-Spouse Transfers

It's also important to remember that, if you are UK domiciled but your spouse is a non-UK domiciliary, the usual IHT exemption for transfers between spouses will not apply and the tax-free amount will be reduced to £55,000. Anything above this would be treated as a 'potentially exempt transfer' for inheritance tax purposes.

This is important because if you planned to make use of your nil rate band (currently £325,000) on a transfer to children and leave the remaining estate to your spouse, you could end up with a big inheritance tax bill.

In this case, you would have to make sure that overseas assets are transferred to your spouse as soon as possible to ensure you survive for seven years after the date of the gift (thereby making it exempt from inheritance tax).

As mentioned earlier, the Government is consulting on increasing the amount of the £55,000 exemption from April 2013. This may then put transfers from UK domiciliaries to their non-domiciled spouses on a similar footing for inheritance tax purposes as other inter-spouse transfers.

Non-Resident Spouse

As well as having a spouse who is non-UK domiciled, you could have a spouse who is non-UK resident, even though you are UK resident. For example, one spouse could work overseas while the other remains in the UK.

As non-UK residents they are largely outside the UK tax system. In many cases it's only if they have UK business assets or property investments that there is any tax at all.

If a couple have significant assets it often pays for the non-resident spouse to hold them so that they can be sold in the future free of UK capital gains tax. This applies to both UK and overseas assets. The only caveat is that if the assets are acquired before the non-resident spouse leaves the UK, he or she would need to remain non-UK resident for at least five complete tax years to avoid capital gains tax forever.

In terms of UK shares, having a non-UK resident spouse is very attractive and is something that one of the UK's most successful businessmen, Philip Green, has used to his advantage. He's a UK resident but his wife is resident in Monaco. Dividends from the UK companies he runs are paid to his wife who is the shareholder and, because she's non-UK resident, they're completely tax free. In addition – and in practice this is an important point – because she's a resident of Monaco, which is a tax haven, there is also no overseas tax.

If your spouse is non-UK resident there's no point paying dividends to her – that would be taxed in the UK at 25% (or higher if she's in the 'Super' tax band) – only to be taxed at a higher rate in another country. It's critical to find out the tax rate applying in the other country. If your spouse can obtain residence overseas in a tax haven of some description, you'll stand the best chance of significantly lowering your tax bill.

Property investors are also well advised to put property assets in their spouse's name to avoid capital gains tax on a future disposal.

In terms of income tax, a non-resident is exempt from tax on non-UK rental income. Therefore, if overseas rental properties are held by the non-resident spouse, income tax can be avoided in full, even if the rental income is subsequently transferred into a UK bank account. (Unlike the position for non-UK domiciliaries above, who would be taxed if the cash was brought into the UK.)

The only tax that would not be directly affected by non-resident status is inheritance tax. To avoid this, the overseas resident spouse also has to obtain non-UK domicile status.

Transfers between Spouses

Where spouses are UK resident there is not normally any rush to transfer assets as you can transfer free of tax pretty much up until the time you decide to sell. Does this apply to transfers between a UK resident and a non-UK resident? Revenue and Customs and the courts have both looked at this issue and agreed that just because one spouse is non-UK resident does not mean that the exemption for inter-spouse transfers should not be available.

Example

Neil has a UK property with a £500,000 gain. His wife is working in Cyprus and is a tax resident there. He transfers the property to his wife who then sells it. As she's a non-UK resident the gain is exempt from capital gains tax provided she spends more than five years abroad. She can then pass the proceeds into a joint account and effectively 'gift' some of these to her husband. In this case, the property gain would also be exempt from Cyprus tax.

You would need to be careful to ensure that ownership is actually transferred and that your spouse really is non-UK resident. As well as this, a non-resident spouse is also outside the scope of many of the anti-avoidance provisions. Therefore offshore companies and trusts could be formed more effectively, for example to hold property investments or even shares. As the spouse is non-resident, showing that any overseas company is controlled from outside the UK should be pretty straightforward.

11.10 PERSONAL SERVICE COMPANIES

With the advent of email and the internet many people trading through UK companies are wanting to move abroad. One way for them to 'have their cake and eat it' is to use an offshore employment company.

Using this they would move overseas and become an employee of the offshore company. The offshore company would charge the UK trading company for the services provided to the UK company.

The UK company should be able to claim this expense as a tax deduction and the offshore company would receive income on which no tax would be payable. Funds could then be extracted from the offshore company by way of a dividend.

Multinationals use this on a larger scale and use offshore employment companies as a vehicle to provide expatriate staff, who work outside both their home country and the offshore jurisdiction, with almost tax-free remuneration.

Example

Paddy runs his own business through a UK company (Paddy Ltd). He is fed up with the British climate and taxes and decides to move overseas.

He settles in the Bahamas and establishes a company in Panama. He still provides services for Paddy Ltd and invoices the company accordingly. Assuming he is the only employee, and the company has profits of £200,000 before paying him, he may decide that the market rate for his services is £150,000 and raise an invoice for this amount from the Panamanian company.

The UK company's taxable profits will be reduced to £50,000, and the £150,000 received by the Panamanian company will not be taxed.

An alternative scenario would be for Paddy to remain an employee of the UK company and perform his duties overseas.

As discussed previously, a non-UK resident individual performing employment duties offshore will not be subject to UK income tax. National insurance should also not be due provided the individual is not UK ordinarily resident. As above, the company should also be allowed a tax deduction for the salary paid.

Note that in both of these situations it is absolutely essential that a market rate is used. HMRC has some complex rules known as the transfer pricing rules that could otherwise apply.

11.11 TRANSFER PRICING RULES

These rules apply where a UK resident is dealing with a non-resident and are intended primarily to prevent companies from manipulating prices to reduce UK taxable profits.

Without these rules it would be easy for a multinational group to arrange for its overseas companies to charge increased amounts for parts, stock or services so as to reduce taxable profits in the UK.

Therefore when a UK resident is dealing with offshore entities, an 'arm's length' rate must be used. This means that if you move offshore and invoice a UK company or charge a salary, the rate you charge must be the same as what would be charged by an unconnected third party providing those services.

You would also need to retain evidence of the third party rate, in case HMRC ever enquires into the matter.

Under self assessment it is for the company to establish and support the fact that an arm's length basis is used. However, HMRC accepts that there may be circumstances where establishing the arm's length rate will be difficult. The transfer pricing provisions therefore provide for a procedure known as 'advance pricing agreements' (APAs).

An APA is a written agreement between a business and HMRC which determines a method for resolving transfer pricing issues in advance of a tax return being made.

It's important to adhere to the provisions of the APA as not only are there potential penalties at stake, but the tax authorities could also restrict the deduction the UK company can claim if it is felt that you have charged an excessive amount.

Advanced offshore arrangements should be carefully considered. They frequently involve a complex interaction of many taxation issues, and professional advice will need to be taken.

11.12 TYPES OF OFFSHORE ENTITY

When looking at the various options available to you to structure your affairs you'll find that there are a number of different entities – both onshore and offshore – that can be used. It can be difficult to understand the differences between the various options so we'll look briefly at each.

UK Limited Company (Ltd)

This is your bog standard company used by traders and investors. It can be used to hold pretty much all assets and can carry out most activities.

When you form the company you'll need to provide some details to both Companies House and later HMRC. Note that any UK incorporated company is automatically classed as UK resident and is therefore taxed in the UK on its worldwide income.

UK Ltd companies are very cheap to form and ongoing administration is not too onerous. You'll need to file annual accounts in a suitable format, and also submit the annual return (which contains details of the company and shareholders).

In terms of asset protection it can be a good way to hold assets separately although, as we've seen, the courts can ignore the company where the arrangement looks like a sham, so you'll need to ensure that there is commercial substance.

If you're looking to trade overseas, a UK company has the advantage of looking highly professional and would not draw attention to your activities, unlike companies registered in certain tax havens. Therefore using a UK Ltd nominee company is popular, to combine a professional front with minimising taxes.

The Ltd company is separate from its shareholders. It can therefore sue or be sued in its own name and will be treated for tax purposes separately from its directors and shareholders. One of the main purposes of forming a Ltd company can be to minimise UK taxes.

UK companies pay UK corporation tax as opposed to income tax and for most this will mean paying corporation tax at 20% as opposed to 40% income tax. Provided only limited profits are extracted from the company (for example, only enough to use up the basic-rate tax band) there would be no further tax to pay. Given that income tax is as high as 50% for high earners (reducing to 45% from April 2013), using a company can have significant tax advantages.

The benefits of using a company will be even greater in the years ahead, as corporation tax is coming down from 25% to 22% for larger companies over the next two years.

UK Limited Liability Partnership (LLP)

This is a cross between a Ltd company and a normal partnership. It was primarily introduced for the large professional firms that carried on a trade as a partnership (for example, lawyers, accountants and surveyors) but who wanted the benefit of limited liability protection.

Therefore an LLP allows the members to protect their personal assets from any creditors, but for tax purposes it is treated just like any other partnership. The LLP will be taxed on a 'pass through' basis with each partner being treated as owning a share in the partnership assets. The profits of the partnership would then be attributed to the partners, irrespective of whether the partners actually take their share of the profits out of the partnership.

For asset protection purposes it offers pretty much the same protection as a Ltd company. In tax terms the tax liability will depend on the partners' residence and other taxable income.

If an LLP is used with a mixture of UK and overseas partners, it would be only the UK partners that would be taxed in the UK, with the overseas partners being taxed in their country of residence. Where there are mixed residence partnerships an LLP may therefore be preferred to a UK company. Mixed residence partnerships also offer certain capital gains tax advantages (covered in the next chapter).

International Business Company (IBC)

This is the name typically given to an offshore company that has been formed outside the UK. There are three main reasons that an IBC may be used.

- To avoid UK taxes

- To hide assets

- To trade overseas, either by UK or overseas residents

Rather than using a simple offshore bank account, many people use an offshore account with the account holder being an IBC – the aim being to sever the link between the individual and the offshore assets.

As with UK companies, IBCs can be used for practically any purpose, including holding overseas property and shares, bank accounts and other assets.

Unlike UK companies, an IBC usually has much lower disclosure requirements with hardly any form filling, no annual accounts or returns and no annual general meeting. It's usually also exempt from local taxes if set up in the correct jurisdiction.

Bearer Share Companies

There are a number of jurisdictions (such as the British Virgin Islands) that permit you to form a special bearer share company. This will cost you more than a standard company – but what benefit do you get for the extra cash?

A normal company lists the owner of the shares on the share certificates and when you want to transfer ownership of the shares you need to notify Companies House.

A bearer share company is totally different. The owner of the company is the person who happens to be holding the share certificate. This means that, provided you do not have the bearer certificates in your possession, you can state that you don't legally own a particular company.

Note the company will still need to pay tax on any profits generated. The only real benefit is in terms of privacy. It would make it more difficult for anyone to argue that you owned a company if bearer shares were used.

Limited Liability Company (LLC)

LLCs are available in a number of jurisdictions, although the United States LLCs (in particular, the Delaware LLC) are the most popular. The LLC is similar to the UK LLP, although there are some important differences.

An LLC is a cross between the UK's LLP and a company. Unlike an LLP an LLC can opt to be taxed as a corporation in many jurisdictions and would therefore be subject to corporate tax on its profits.

Individuals who own an interest in an LLC are known as 'members' as opposed to shareholders.

The LLC structure is known to be very flexible and reporting requirements are not onerous, with few requirements to keep minutes or have records of formal resolutions (although this is often advisable).

LLCs also benefit from limited liability protection, thus ensuring that your personal assets are kept separate from your business assets.

Unlike an LLP, the minimum number of people needed to form an LLC is one, with a few exceptions. If you did set one up with just one member, this would be akin to a one man limited company, albeit with low disclosure and documentary requirements.

HMRC usually classes LLCs as 'opaque' entities for UK tax purposes. This means that they are treated as companies and have a separate legal personality. They can also be classed as having ordinary share capital for UK tax purposes providing certificates of LLC membership interests are issued.

Note that for US tax purposes LLCs are by default classed as transparent and taxed like sole traders or partnerships (ie with the LLC members directly taxed on the profits).

182

Trusts

Trusts were traditionally one of the most popular entities for holding assets. They were particularly useful as they allowed an individual to legally give away assets but still exercise an element of control over them (as a trustee) and in some cases benefit from the assets (as a beneficiary).

In terms of avoiding UK taxes they are much less attractive now than they used to be due to the number of anti-avoidance provisions that operate to negate the tax benefits.

Offshore trusts would usually be used in combination with another entity such as an IBC or a foundation. Typically the trust would be used to hold the shares of an IBC. Alternatively, if a foundation structure was used, the trust could be the beneficiary of the foundation.

Foundations

The use of foundations has gained in popularity over the past few years, given its unique characteristics. The foundation is essentially a cross between a trust and a company because it's a separate legal entity that doesn't have owners.

Foundations are useful because they have a separate legal personality. Therefore when applying for an offshore bank account, it is often necessary to state the beneficial owners. If a foundation is used it is the foundation itself that is the beneficial owner. Foundations are popular primarily for asset protection purposes.

In UK tax terms, they'd be likely to be treated in a similar way to a company.

Protected Cell Companies (PCCs)

Protected cell companies are something of a new development. There are very few jurisdictions that permit them (including Guernsey, Bermuda and Mauritius) and although aimed at big business and the structuring of finance for multinational companies, they could be tailored to a smaller operation if required.

A protected cell company is a company that is split up into different sections. Each section is separate from all the others and rather than simply transferring assets to the company, you transfer assets to the particular cell of the company. Each cell is independent and separate from every other cell.

Therefore, rather than holding assets in separate companies, you could establish one PCC and put different assets in each cell. In terms of any creditors each cell would need to be approached separately and the assets of one cell could not be used to satisfy liabilities of another cell.

They're principally asset protection tools and, given the right circumstances, for example if there is a diverse range of assets involved, they could be useful.

UK Tax Treatment of Overseas Entities

If you're planning on using an overseas trust or company it's essential to ensure that you know exactly how it will be treated by the UK taxman.

There are broadly speaking two ways in which an overseas entity could be classed. It could either be classed like a UK partnership or LLP (known as 'transparent') or like a UK limited liability company (known as 'opaque').

The difference is crucial, as it will impact directly on how any overseas profits are taxed in the UK.

In the case of a transparent entity, such as an LLP or a partnership, the profits are taxed in the hands of the members. In other words, the members are treated as earning the profits, irrespective of whether the profits are actually paid out to them.

An opaque entity, on the other hand, is treated as earning the profits. Therefore the members are only taxed on the amounts they actually extract from the company.

In order to decide whether an overseas entity is transparent or opaque there are a number of tests that the UK tax authorities will apply. In particular, they will look at the following:

- Does the overseas entity have a separate legal existence?

- Does the entity issue share capital or something that is similar to share capital?

- Is the business carried on by the entity itself or by the members who have an interest in it?

- Are the members entitled to share in the entity's profits as they arise or does the amount of profits to which they are entitled depend on a decision of the entity or its members (for example, in a UK company the dividend needs to be declared by the directors)?

- Who is responsible for any business debts – the entity or the members?

- Do the entity's assets belong to the entity or to the members?

Of key importance will be the impact of foreign law and in particular the authorities will look at the distribution of profits from the entity and who actually carries out the business. Essentially it's a case of looking at where the true rights of ownership and control arise.

However, rather than assess each overseas entity on a case by case basis, the UK taxman has already looked at a long list of foreign entities and determined their UK treatment.

While this should be regarded as a general overview only, I've highlighted the UK treatment in Appendix II.

Therefore if you're considering using an offshore entity it's important to try to establish whether it enjoys opaque or transparent tax treatment.

11.13 OVERSEAS TRADING

If you want to do business in another country, the options you have include:

- Incorporate a new company offshore and use it to carry out the overseas business, or

- Establish a branch of the existing UK company and carry out the trade via the branch.

Note that in physical terms the two would look more or less identical. For example, there could be overseas premises, staff and equipment.

The main difference would be in the ownership. If the overseas trade was owned by the UK company, it would be a branch. If it was owned by an offshore company, it could be a subsidiary.

Deciding whether to use a branch or subsidiary will have significant implications on how the profits from the overseas trade will be taxed.

Old Rules

Prior to 19th July 2011, the main difference between a branch and subsidiary is that the profits of a branch will be classed as part of the UK company's taxable profits, along with its UK trading profits.

The branch profits will usually be separated from the UK trading income if the branch is actually controlled from overseas, and therefore it could be taxed as income from an overseas 'possession', as opposed to trading income. This difference is not all that important, however, and the key point is that all profits of the overseas branch will be subject to UK corporation tax.

By contrast, if an overseas subsidiary is used, and provided the company is non-UK resident, the profits of the overseas subsidiary should not be subject to UK corporation tax.

The company will be non-UK resident if it is not incorporated in the UK and its central management and control is overseas.

In addition, provided the overseas company does not fall within the controlled foreign company provisions (see below) the only time that the UK company will be subject to corporation tax is when the overseas company declares a dividend.

This would therefore give the UK company an element of control over when it incurs a UK tax charge (for example, during an accounting period of otherwise low income).

Another key difference is that if a branch is used and it sustains a loss, this can often be offset against other UK trading profits. If you use an overseas subsidiary and the subsidiary incurs a loss, the opportunities for it to utilise its loss are restricted.

The fact that losses are given more flexible relief in a branch means that, where an overseas operation is expected to incur losses in the first few years of trading, it is often advisable to initially trade overseas using a branch (with full relief for losses in the UK) and then transfer the trade to an overseas subsidiary when it is about to become profitable (to eliminate UK tax on the profits).

Finally, if you use a subsidiary, it will be classed as an 'associated company' which would reduce the tax bands for calculating the UK company's corporation tax. In other words, a higher corporation tax rate may be payable on a slice of the company's profits.

New Rules

As of 19th July 2011 there has been a significant change to the tax treatment of foreign branches of UK companies. If an (irrevocable) election is made, all profits and losses can remain permanently outside the scope of UK corporation tax. There are certain conditions that have to be met but if an election is made:

- The election has to apply to all foreign branches.

- Capital gains and income profits and losses are covered.

- Assets utilised in the overseas branch are, for tax purposes, transferred to it from the UK company at a no gain/no loss value at the outset of the election taking effect.

Inevitably there are detailed anti-avoidance provisions to prevent abuse. Certain types of businesses are excluded from the new rules, including:

- Long term insurance businesses, being primarily life assurance and permanent health insurance,

- Companies which derive their income mainly from making investments,

- Certain international air transport and shipping companies, and

- The profits of close companies which stem from capital gains.

Additionally, smaller companies can only make the new election if their foreign branches are situated in territories that have a double taxation treaty with the UK that includes a non-discrimination clause.

A small company is, broadly, one with no more than 50 staff and with either annual turnover or a balance sheet of less than €10 million.

So if you have a small company and are setting up a branch in a country with which the UK has a treaty, you would need to weigh up the fact that making the election is irrevocable, not just for that branch but for all future branches.

Losses will not be allowable for offset against UK profits but branch profits will not be taxed.

If, however, the foreign jurisdiction levied tax on the profits that would fully cover any UK liability under the double tax relief provisions, it may be preferable not to make the election. This would then ensure that losses were still available.

11.14 UK CONTROLLED FOREIGN COMPANY (CFC) RULES

I mentioned above that the UK company would not be charged tax on the profits of the overseas non-UK resident subsidiary... provided the UK CFC rules don't apply. The CFC rules are therefore very important for any company that wants to set up an overseas subsidiary.

If the CFC rules apply, the UK company will have to pay tax on the overseas company's profits, provided the percentage of profits apportioned is at least 25%.

You should note that the UK CFC regime will not apply if you are an individual owning an overseas company.

Before falling within the CFC rules a company would firstly need to meet the definition of a 'controlled foreign company'.

A CFC is defined as:

- A non-UK resident company, and

- A company controlled from the UK, and

- A company subject to overseas tax which is less than 75% of the equivalent UK tax.

Therefore the CFC provisions are going to apply to overseas companies established in countries with low tax. What you would need to do is calculate the company's profits and find out what the overseas tax charge is.

You would then calculate the UK tax liability and, if the overseas tax paid is less than three-quarters of the UK tax, the overseas company could fall within the CFC provisions.

Before getting into the nitty-gritty of the new regime applying from 2012, it's worthwhile noting that the big news for small companies is that the de-minimis profits limit will be raised from £50,000 per annum to £500,000 per annum. Most small companies will therefore fall outside the CFC rules.

The New CFC Rules

New rules for controlled foreign companies (CFCs) are to be introduced in the 2012 Finance Bill.

The aims of the new CFC regime, as laid out in the latest consultation document, are to:

- Target and impose a CFC charge on artificially diverted profits so that UK profits are fairly taxed,

- Exempt foreign profits where there is no artificial diversion of UK profits, and

- Not tax profits arising from genuine economic activities undertaken offshore.

Overview of New Regime

The new regime is targeted at situations that pose the highest risk of artificial diversion of UK profits. A proportionate approach is adopted so that, where a CFC charge applies, it will only apply to those profits which have been diverted artificially from the UK. Genuine foreign profits are exempt from the charge.

The regime also seeks to recognise that most CFCs are held for genuine commercial reasons and do not pose a risk to the UK tax base. Consequently a number of exemptions will apply, including a general purposes exemption providing companies with the opportunity to demonstrate that they have not artificially diverted profits from the UK.

The new regime will in many ways operate in a similar way to the existing regime. It will identify low taxed foreign companies controlled from the UK.

The existence of a number of exemptions will remove from the CFC regime those CFCs that do not artificially divert profits away from the UK. The exemptions, however, are being modernised.

Three-Step Approach

The new regime will follow a three-step approach:

- Identifying CFCs

- Exempting CFCs that pose a low risk to the UK tax base

- Calculating a CFC charge when profits have been artificially diverted from the UK

The first step is to identify a CFC. For the purposes of the new regime, a CFC is a company that is under UK control, is resident outside the UK and has profits that are taxed at a lower effective rate than if the company were resident in the UK.

Having identified a CFC, the second step is to see whether one or more of the exemptions apply, including:

- **Excluded territories exemption**. HMRC will publish a list of those jurisdictions where they are happy that the local corporation tax will be no less than 75% of the UK equivalent liability. Any companies resident in these jurisdictions will not be CFCs.

- **Low profits exemption**. If the overseas company's profits are less than £500,000 it will not be a CFC.

- **Low profit margin exemption**. This exemption applies to CFCs whose accounting profits are less than 10% of their costs. Cost cannot include any related party expenditure.

Safe Harbours

Next we move onto the business trading income "safe harbour". Here the CFC needs to meet a variety of tests.

These include having:

- Business premises available locally

- Incurring no more than 20% of overall expenditure on supplies from UK sources

- Invoicing no more than 20% of total turnover to UK customers

- Limited connection to UK orientated intellectual property rights, and

- The management costs of the CFC being at least 80% incurred outside the UK.

There is an exemption for CFCs that only let property in the foreign jurisdiction.

There is a new exemption for finance companies set up in low tax jurisdictions which meet a number of criteria. This reduces the rate of UK corporation tax that might be levied down to just 5.75%.

There will also be a new 'gateway test' which will allow companies to be ruled out of the CFC regime.

When Will the New CFC Rules Apply?

As part of the consultation process, the Government consulted on the appropriate start date for the new regime. The earliest the regime will come into force is for accounting periods beginning on or after the date of Royal Assent of the 2012 Finance Bill.

It is important that any UK company planning related to using an overseas subsidiary is carried out very carefully to ensure that it does not fall foul of the CFC provisions – doing so would eliminate the benefits of using an offshore company.

11.15 UK CORPORATION TAX PLANNING AFTER YOU'VE LEFT THE UK

If you trade via a UK company, the general rule is that it is subject to UK corporation tax, even if the controlling directors or shareholders are non-UK resident.

As the company is a UK company it is classed as UK resident and is subject to UK corporation tax.

In terms of actually extracting cash from the company, this can be easily achieved by paying dividends.

If the shareholders are non-resident they can effectively receive dividends free of UK income tax.

However, the profits out of which the dividends are paid will still have been subject to UK corporation tax.

If the aim is to reduce the corporation tax on the company profits you need to look at additional options.

Salary/Bonus

The simplest way to reduce the company's profits is to pay salary or bonuses to employees/directors. The salary/bonus would not be subject to income tax, provided the directors are non-resident and carry out their employment duties overseas (aside from any incidental UK duties).

The company is permitted a tax deduction for all expenses incurred "wholly and exclusively" for the purposes of the trade.

In order for the company to substantiate a tax deduction for salary or bonus payments it would need to be linked to a benefit received by the company and for the purposes of its trade. This usually means that the salary/bonus payments need to be:

- Genuine services provided by the employees/directors to the company, and

- Calculated at an arm's length rate.

Essentially you would want to be able to argue that the company would make these payments even if the employees/directors were otherwise unconnected with the company (e.g. not shareholders).

You could, for instance, look at paying both a market value salary for the duties undertaken by non-resident directors, as well as a bonus arrangement related to their specific fields of responsibility.

Note that employment income can be subject to UK national insurance (13.8% paid by the employer and up to 12% paid by the employee). Reciprocal agreements with other countries, as well as EU agreements, can affect your national insurance liability. However, long-term emigrants can usually receive salary/bonus payments free of UK national insurance.

Offshore Company

The other option would be to use an offshore structure, such as an offshore company, and recharge amounts to the UK company. In terms of the company itself you would need to ensure:

- It is controlled and managed from overseas. There should be no issue with this if the controlling directors and shareholders are non-resident.

- It has no UK trade (as even if non-resident, profits from a UK trade could still be within the scope of UK tax). The location of the trade is usually where the key revenue generating activities are undertaken.

The simplest way to use an offshore company is for the directors to provide services via the offshore company to the UK company. This is a form of service company. Similar considerations apply as above (ie in terms of transfer pricing) and you would need to ensure that the rates charged for the services provided are market related.

The offshore company would receive the receipts free of UK tax. The UK company would obtain a tax deduction for the payments.

If you were seeking to transfer part of the trade of a UK company to an offshore company, this could avoid UK tax (subject to the transfer of any goodwill – see below). The offshore company would recharge for the services to the UK company which would be free of tax in the offshore company. A British Virgin Islands or Isle of Man company is often used for this purpose.

HMRC usually accepts that a service company used to employ staff, own or lease business premises or provide other administrative services is genuine, assuming that the company recharges the UK company at an appropriate mark up (eg 10-15%).

Another option would be to use an offshore holding company. You would achieve this by using a share for share exchange to place the new offshore company as the holding company of the UK company. A management recharge from the UK to the offshore company would be deductible for corporation tax purposes but again you would need to ensure that it related to genuine services provided by the offshore company to the UK company. A management recharge of 100% of the profits, for instance, would not be acceptable.

Goodwill

An important issue on a transfer of any aspect of the trade would be whether there was a transfer of goodwill from the UK company. The transfer of the trade from the UK company to the offshore company would be a disposal for capital gains purposes. This isn't a specific rule that applies to transfers to offshore companies but rather is a general rule that applies to the transfer of any assets out of a company.

Therefore, irrespective of the disposal consideration that is actually transferred from the offshore company to the UK company, the capital gain realised by the UK company would be based on the market value of the assets transferred. You would therefore need to value the assets transferred to the offshore company. This would include plant/machinery and any land or property but usually goodwill is the largest asset transferred.

However, if the value of the goodwill is represented by the personal services carried out by the directors, they may be able to argue that it is effectively personal goodwill. If this is the case, they may be able to argue that there is no disposal for CGT purposes.

Aside from this, a transfer of back office operations with a recharge to the UK company would usually be acceptable.

In terms of actually transferring the revenue generating activities, the best option may be to undertake new activities in the offshore company, where there could be no argument of a transfer of goodwill. The profits may then arise free of UK tax in the offshore company.

Chapter 12

Investing in UK Property:
A Case Study

It is useful to consolidate some of the issues covered in previous chapters and consider a typical scenario, where a UK non-resident and non-domiciled individual wishes to purchase a UK property.

Jack is resident and domiciled in Spain. He has relatives in the UK and is interested in purchasing a property here because (a) he wants somewhere to stay when he visits and (b) he has heard that UK property prices are set to rise.

The question is, how from a tax perspective should he structure the purchase?

There are broadly two ways to buy the property:

- By using direct ownership, or
- Using some form of intermediary like a trust or company.

12.1 DIRECT OWNERSHIP

Capital Gains Tax

From a capital gains tax perspective direct ownership is potentially attractive:

- The Principal Private Residence (PPR) relief operates to exempt a gain on the disposal of an individual's main residence. Even if the property is not, on the facts, Jack's main residence, he could certainly submit an election to have it treated as his main residence.

- As he is non-resident, he would not in any case be liable to UK capital gains tax on the disposal of any assets.

Inheritance Tax

The inheritance tax position is, however, not as good. The holding of property in the UK would mean that Jack has a UK estate and, as well as probate being required on his death, the house would be subject to inheritance tax to the extent that the value exceeds the £325,000 nil rate band. As the value of the property is expected to rise rapidly, this could result in a significant tax bill were he to die while still owning the asset. There are, however, a number of methods available to Jack to reduce or eliminate any inheritance tax charge:

Use of Multiple Ownership

The property could be acquired in multiple ownership. For example, Jack, his wife and children could all own the property jointly.

Provided the individuals have no other UK assets, it is likely that each share will be below the nil rate band.

In order to avoid problems with the 'gift with reservation of benefit' legislation, it is necessary to gift cash to the family members, which they can then use to purchase their shares of the property.

The gift with reservation of benefit (GROB) provisions apply to property in particular, where an interest in a property is given away, yet the person gifting the interest still continues to reside in the property. For inheritance tax purposes, the whole value of the property is still regarded as included in the occupier's estate for inheritance tax purposes.

Gifting of Property

Another solution would be to gift cash to a younger member of the family who can then make the acquisition. The gift will be exempt from inheritance tax, provided the person making the gift survives seven years. The above GROB rules would not apply as the gift was a cash gift.

197

The UK pre-owned assets tax charge should also not be relevant if Jack is non-UK resident.

The property will then belong to the donee (the younger family member) and if the donee were to die, it would be included in his estate for inheritance tax purposes.

Mortgages

The value of an individual's estate is essentially the market value of the assets at the date of death, less any liabilities outstanding at the date of death.

It is therefore possible to effectively reduce any inheritance tax charge to zero by obtaining a substantial loan against the value of the property. Provided the mortgage reduces the 'net value' of the property to below the nil rate band (currently £325,000), there will be no inheritance tax payable.

The mortgage funds obtained can be invested overseas and any interest return would then be exempt from UK income tax provided the interest income is not remitted to the UK.

12.2   USING A TRUST TO OWN THE PROPERTY

Capital Gains Tax

The Principal Private Residence relief is extended to situations where a beneficiary is entitled to occupy a house under the terms of a trust deed. In these circumstances, the trustees would be able to claim PPR relief when they sell the property.

In the case of a non-UK domiciliary, as the trustees are non-resident they would not, in any case, be liable to UK capital gains tax.

It would only be if the settlor of the trust (or his close family) was also a beneficiary and became UK resident that the gains of the trust could be attributed to him under the anti-avoidance provisions.

Inheritance Tax

The trust will be subject to special inheritance tax rules. One of the key implications is that it could be subject to an inheritance tax charge every 10 years starting with the date of commencement.

12.3 USING AN OFFSHORE COMPANY

The property could be owned by a non-resident company. In this case the non-domiciliary would own the shares in the company.

As the shares are non-UK property, they would be exempt from inheritance tax. Key risks with this are:

- The company's residence position may be closely scrutinised by the taxman and it may be difficult to show that the central management and control is exercised outside the UK, particularly if all directors are UK resident and the asset of the company is a UK property. If HMRC is able to successfully argue that the company is UK resident, any gain on the disposal of the property would be subject to UK corporation tax and no PPR relief would be available.

- In addition, on a disposal of the shares in the company, no capital gains tax would be payable by Jack provided he remained non-resident. If he was UK resident, he may not be charged to UK CGT provided the proceeds were retained outside the UK and he was subject to the remittance basis, as he's a non-UK domiciliary.

12.4 TAX PLANNING FOR NON-RESIDENTS OWNING UK PROPERTY INVESTMENT COMPANIES

Many individuals hold their UK properties in a UK company.

When these individuals move overseas and lose UK residence they will often hold onto their property company.

The company has to pay UK corporation tax on any rental profits. However, the shareholder can extract the remaining profits free of UK income tax/withholding tax and can always sell the shares in the company free of capital gains tax.

If the company sells the properties, however, corporation tax will have to be paid on the capital gains.

One important issue is financing the properties. This could come from either the UK or overseas.

UK financing is often preferred. The UK company would obtain a corporation tax deduction for the interest, but the shareholder could then extract the funds which could be invested overseas free of UK income tax. If the shareholder is resident in a tax haven it may be possible to completely avoid income tax on the interest generated. This is potentially a win-win scenario with the interest being tax deductible in the UK company and reinvested overseas free of tax.

If financing is obtained from overseas the risk is that the tax deduction at source rules could apply. These can require tax to be deducted by the payer where the interest is from a UK source but the payment is made overseas. In the case of a UK company paying interest overseas, the net result is that the UK company may need to account for 20% income tax on the interest paid overseas.

The key issue is where the 'source' of the interest is. Revenue and Customs would look at a number of factors to determine whether the interest has a UK source:

- The residence of the debtor (this is usually taken to be the place where the debt will be enforced),
- The source from which interest is paid,
- Where the interest is paid, and
- The nature and location of any security for the debt.

If the loan was made to a UK company from overseas and in respect of UK property it would be likely that the interest would have a UK source and as such be subject to the deduction of tax at source rules. Therefore whilst it would be deductible for the UK company when calculating its taxable profits, there could be a 20% income tax liability on the interest.

The options to avoid this are limited if the interest is paid overseas. A payment to a UK bank avoids these issues.

The main option to reduce withholding tax on interest paid overseas would be to rely on a double tax treaty. These provide for an exemption or reduction in UK tax deducted at source depending on the particular agreement that the UK has with the country in question. You could therefore ensure that the deduction at source from the UK was eliminated.

Transferring Properties to an Offshore Company

Another option would be to transfer the properties to an offshore company. The main tax issue here would be having to pay corporation tax on any capital gain made up to the date of transfer.

So this strategy works best if there has only been a nominal increase in the value of the properties.

A transfer overseas could, however, shelter you from paying tax on any future gains. If the properties remain in a UK company, any increase in value will be subject to UK corporation tax at a rate of up to 24% from April 2012.

If the properties are held by a non-resident, UK tax on the gain could be avoided. The rental income would fall within the non resident landlord scheme and an application would need to be made to receive the interest gross (without UK income tax deducted on the rental income).

Income tax (note not corporation tax) would be assessed via a self assessment return. Any interest paid to a non resident lender could still be claimed as a tax deduction in calculating the UK taxable profits.

Another benefit of holding the properties via a non UK company would be if the shareholder has lost UK domicile. A non UK domiciliary would be subject to UK inheritance tax on the value of the UK shares if it was not a trading company.

By contrast a non domiciliary wouldn't be subject to inheritance tax on the value of overseas shares if the UK properties were held via an offshore company.

12.5 CONCLUSION

Deciding how a non-domiciliary should own UK property is clearly not a straightforward decision.

Much will depend on the particular circumstances and your personal preferences. For example, you may be more anxious to avoid capital gains tax than inheritance tax.

To a certain extent the simplest route – direct ownership – offers some important tax advantages provided potential inheritance tax can be avoided in some way, for example, by using debt.

Chapter 13

Becoming a Tax Nomad

Just as it is possible to be resident in more than one country, it is also possible to be resident in none. Such individuals are commonly known as 'tax nomads'.

If you become a tax nomad you would still be liable for income tax on any income generated within a particular country, but *capital gains tax* usually depends on the concept of residence.

In order to achieve your objective and pay no capital gains tax, you will need to ensure that you have a thorough understanding of the relevant countries' domestic tax laws, as well as the impact of any double taxation treaties.

The definition of residence varies significantly. Some countries, such as the UK and Ireland, have an objective test, which is determined in part by the number of days spent within the country.

Other countries, such as France and Germany, have a more subjective test that is based on where an individual's 'centre of economic interest' is located or the place of 'habitual abode'.

Example

Jack spends his time during the tax year 2012/13 as follows:

- *127 days in Ireland,*
- *84 days a year in the UK,*
- *110 days in the USA,*
- *The remainder of the year on holiday in the Maldives.*

He should not be resident in any of the above countries for tax purposes and this would allow him to avoid a potentially large gain on a disposal of his investment property. Note that in terms of establishing non UK residence it would be vital that he severed as many ties with the UK as possible, including selling/leasing UK property, taking his family with him and having overseas business interests.

Moving abroad may offer an opportunity to wash out gains in your investment portfolio tax-free, since it may be possible to arrange your move so that for a period you are 'resident nowhere'.

For example, if you move to Spain and leave the UK on 5th April 2012 and travel via France, arriving in Spain on 10th April 2012, any capital gains you realise during the four-day 'tax holiday' between these dates could be free of capital gains tax (unless you resume tax residence in the UK within five years), providing you avoid being classed as Spanish resident for 2012.

Whilst becoming a tax nomad may not be a suitable option long term, it could prove useful for one or two years – it allows you to structure your affairs before taking up residence in a country of your choice. The general rules relating to losing your UK residence still apply though, and the fact that you don't have an overseas country of residence can make it more difficult to establish non-UK resident status, unless you have strong evidence to support the permanent departure from the UK.

A safer option if you're relying on this to avoid UK capital gains tax may be to establish treaty residence in a country that has a double tax treaty with the UK, but that also doesn't tax the gain. This should then make it much easier to avoid tax on the disposal.

Chapter 14

Double Tax Treaties

14.1 HOW DOUBLE TAX TREATIES WORK

The rules detailed earlier in this guide explain the concepts of 'residence', 'ordinary residence' and 'domicile' and identify when an individual will be liable to pay UK tax as a result of being resident or ordinarily resident in this country.

But an individual may also be regarded as resident in another country according to its tax laws. This is where double tax treaties come into play.

A double tax treaty is essentially an agreement between two countries that will determine which country has the right to tax you in specified situations. The purpose is to avoid double taxation.

The UK has double tax treaties with a number of countries including popular retirement destinations such as Spain, Portugal, Italy and France.

The majority of the UK's double tax treaties are based on the 'standard' provisions in the model treaty of the OECD (Organisation for Economic Cooperation and Development).

This includes a 'tie-breaker' clause that effectively overrides the two countries' domestic laws and makes the individual resident in one country only. The use of this tie-breaker clause can be extremely beneficial, as we'll see shortly.

14.2 WHAT A TYPICAL DTT LOOKS LIKE

As most of the UK DTTs follow the standard OECD model, I'll explain in the paragraphs that follow what some of the most common OECD double tax treaty provisions are actually trying to achieve.

Some of these are self-explanatory but are worth listing in case you ever want to review a DTT on your own.

Article V – Permanent Establishment

This looks at the definition of a permanent establishment. This is crucial for international traders as this will frequently dictate the extent to which overseas trading activities will be taxable in an overseas jurisdiction. Usually a company trading in the other treaty country would only be taxed on the profits in the 'source' country if they are trading from a permanent establishment located there.

Article VI – Income from Real Property

Typically real property is land and property, so this article would cover the treatment of rental income. As the country where the property is located usually has the initial right to tax, the rental income could easily be taxed in both countries.

Most income tax treaties under Article VI will not avoid this by providing an exemption in one of the countries, so instead you'd usually rely on Article XXIV (elimination of double tax article) to provide a tax credit for the overseas tax suffered (see below).

Article XI – Interest

This looks at the position where interest is paid by a resident of one country to a resident of another. The treaty between the two countries would usually look to reduce any withholding taxes (for example, in the case of the UK it would identify if the UK 20% withholding tax would be reduced).

Article XIII – Capital Gains

This is the one that is of most importance for property investors looking to emigrate and sell up. It covers capital gains from the disposal of assets and seeks to reduce the tax dependent on the specific treaty country. In many cases there is a standard provision that capital gains remain taxable only in the owner's country of residence, except for land and property which can also usually be taxed in the country where the property is located. So whilst most expats could be exempt from UK taxes, they could find themselves liable to capital gains tax overseas.

Article XIV – Independent Personal Services

This looks at the taxation of income from self-employed people and again will generally look to whether the individual has a 'fixed base' overseas. If they do, then it's often only the profits generated by this fixed base that can be taxed overseas.

Article XV – Dependent Personal Services

This looks at the taxation of employment income. In many treaties if the income is paid and borne by a foreign employer and the employee is not physically present in the UK for more than 183 days, the income will only be taxable in the employee's country of residence.

Article XXII – Other Income

This looks at the taxation of all other income not addressed elsewhere and usually gives sole taxing rights to the country of residence.

Article XXIV – Elimination of Double Taxation

This provides for double tax relief, so that even if income is taxed twice you'll be able to deduct overseas tax that you've suffered from any UK liability. Although useful, the UK would usually provide for double tax relief anyway, even if there was no treaty in place (under what is known as 'unilateral relief').

Exceptionally, some treaties may also grant an exemption rather than the credit method above.

Article XXVII – Exchange of Information

This is an agreement between the two tax authorities to allow them to share information, mainly to avoid tax evasion. This is the other side to double tax treaties – as well as looking to reduce tax, they are also effectively information exchange agreements.

The terms of double tax treaties can therefore be immensely complex, although on a simple level they can provide for one country to have primary taxing rights over certain sources of income and gains.

The tie-breaker clause that I mentioned earlier is the way that the tax treaty will determine in which of the two countries an individual is resident for treaty purposes.

A typical treaty would provide that:

- If you have a permanent home in one state, you are resident in that state.

- If you have a permanent home in both states, you are resident in the state that is your 'centre of vital interests' – the country in which you have close personal and financial ties.

- If you do not have a permanent home in either state and it is not possible to determine your centre of vital interests, you are resident in the country where you have an 'habitual abode'.

One important point to note is that there are very few low-tax countries that have double tax treaties with the UK. The UK has, however, concluded double tax treaties with the Channel Islands and the Isle of Man, which are low-tax jurisdictions. The UK-Isle of Man double tax treaty is looked at in more detail below.

It is also crucial to note that for the tie-breaker clause to apply, you must be resident in two countries under the terms of each country's domestic laws. The treaty cannot make you resident in a country if you are not already resident under the domestic law of that country.

There is also a tie breaker clause for companies, which usually looks at the country where the 'effective management is carried out'. Before this could apply a company would need to be resident in both treaty countries. For example, in the *Wood v Holden* case mentioned previously, HMRC argued that the Dutch company was UK resident given its central management and control was in the UK.

HMRC also said that under the UK-Netherlands tax treaty the company was UK resident as the effective place of management was not in the Netherlands. However, as the High Court judge ruled that the company was Dutch resident, the treaty provision was not relevant in deciding the company's residence.

Note that I'm not saying that you need to be resident in both treaty countries to obtain the benefits under the treaty, just that the residence tie-breaker rules won't apply unless you are dual resident.

The impact of being treaty resident overseas is that most treaties ensure that you are subject to the overseas tax rules on overseas income.

The other provisions relating to income and gains will usually apply where you have a potential tax charge in both states. Therefore you could be UK resident but if you invest in German property you'll be subject to both countries' capital gains tax regime and will look to the treaty to identify how this deals with the double taxation.

14.3 THE UK-ISLE OF MAN DOUBLE TAX TREATY

The Isle of Man (IOM) has only one Double Taxation Agreement which was entered into with the United Kingdom in 1955 and is very similar to agreements drawn up between the UK and Jersey and Guernsey.

The treaty does not conform to the OECD standard model treaty and is of limited scope. The main features that may be of interest are the following:

- The agreement applies only for income tax purposes (in both the IOM and the UK).

- An individual resident in only one of the two countries is exempt from tax in the other country on personal, including professional, services performed in the other country on behalf of a resident of his own country (but they must be taxed in his own country). In other words, if you are a resident of the IOM and perform services in the UK for a UK resident individual, then provided the income was taxed in the IOM, there would be no UK tax liability.

If these criteria are not met then tax would be payable in both countries, although the tax paid in one country is allowed as a credit against tax due in the other. If you did incur UK tax whilst being an IOM resident, the UK tax paid would be offset against any IOM tax.

Given that UK income tax rates are generally significantly higher then IOM rates, this would extinguish any IOM income tax liability.

It is important to note that capital gains tax is not subject to the double tax treaty.

Why the Isle of Man is So Attractive

Tax rates are much lower in the Isle of Man than in the UK.

For tax year 2012/13 income tax is levied at a rate of only 10% on the first £10,500 of taxable income and 20% on the rest. Individuals also receive a £9,300 personal allowance. Married couples are taxed jointly and receive a personal allowance of £18,600, pay 10% on the first £21,000 of taxable income and 20% on the rest. The Isle of Man has also introduced an income tax cap of £115,000. This means that if you're very wealthy, your maximum income tax charge is restricted to £115,000.

National insurance is levied on employment income at similar rates to the UK. For employees the rate is 11% on income between £118 and £770 per week.

Rates are a form of property tax and are based on a notional house value multiplied by a formula set by the local authority.

There is also VAT, which is charged at the same rate as in the UK.

There is no capital gains tax in the Isle of Man and corporation tax is 0% for many companies.

How to Become Resident in the Isle of Man

There is no general definition of 'residence' or 'ordinary residence' in Manx tax law – these terms are often interpreted in the same way as in English law.

A person will qualify as a resident if he spends a total of six months on the island in any income tax year (April 6th to April 5th). An individual who visits for more than an average of three months each year for four or more consecutive years will also be deemed resident. There is an important short-term residence concession which allows a person who owns a property on the island to spend not more than four months in any two consecutive years in the island and not be liable to Manx income tax.

A new resident is taxed from the date of arrival, while a person who leaves is non-resident from the date of departure. Resident individuals are liable to tax on their worldwide income, non-residents only on income arising on the island.

14.4   USING DOUBLE TAX TREATIES TO SAVE TAX

Before the 2005 Budget it was possible to use certain favourable double tax treaties with countries like Belgium, Portugal and New Zealand to avoid having to leave the UK for five years to avoid capital gains tax.

These treaties superseded the UK domestic tax legislation and allowed only the overseas country to tax gains of residents, thus preventing a UK tax charge, even if the person became UK resident within five years. However, this is no longer possible due to the new anti-avoidance rules. The fact that a double tax treaty exists does not prevent UK Revenue and Customs taxing any gain arising in the tax year of your return.

You would therefore need to actually remain resident overseas for a five-year period for the gain to be exempt from UK capital gains tax.

If this is an option (for example, if the amount of any gain is significant) you could choose a CGT-free destination such as the Isle of Man or the Channel Islands, a complete tax haven such as Monaco, or a country that has specific provisions to exempt gains on overseas property (for example, Cyprus).

After the tax year of disposal, you could then cease to be a resident of this country and travel or establish residence in another country of your choice (for example, Spain). Provided you do not become a UK resident for five complete tax years, you will be exempt from UK CGT. You could return to the UK for visits, although you should keep these to a minimum, especially if you have UK family or property.

Although the use of double tax treaties to avoid UK capital gains tax has decreased, the use of treaties for individuals and companies to avoid income tax or corporation tax is still significant. For example, the permanent establishment provisions of a relevant double tax treaty are very important for international traders as they can actively limit liability to UK taxes for UK traders.

14.5   TREATY RELIEF

Remember that double tax treaties override domestic tax legislation. In the standard OECD model tax treaty, dividends can be taxed in the country of the shareholders residence, usually with a reduced withholding tax in the country where the company is resident.

In this case, you would need to contact Revenue and Customs and apply for treaty relief in order that the exemption or reduction in UK tax can apply. This would then allow a repayment of any tax withheld, and would ensure that no income tax is deducted on future payments.

Claiming treaty relief can be a long process. The form, which can be obtained from Revenue and Customs (www.hmrc.gov.uk/cnr), must be completed and passed to the overseas revenue service. It will then review the information and pass this back to the UK

HMRC where the Centre for Non Residents will issue a certificate granting relief.

14.6   LIVING OR BUYING PROPERTY IN SPAIN

Let's have a look at Spain, a popular destination for potential expats. Whilst Spain does not offer low tax rates, it still remains a popular choice for UK emigrants due to its proximity to the UK, fantastic climate and political stability.

Those who either purchase Spanish assets or acquire Spanish residence will be affected by the local tax regime so it's worth examining in greater detail.

We shall give a brief overview of the Spanish tax regime below. This will highlight the similarities and differences between the two countries, before looking at how the UK-Spain double tax treaty affects matters.

Residence

The extent that you are liable to these taxes will depend on your residence position. You will either be UK resident or Spanish resident (assuming you live and split your time between the UK and Spain).

Residence is important because UK and Spanish residents are taxed on their *worldwide* income and gains, whereas non-residents are only liable to tax on the income arising within that particular country.

For example, non-UK residents are only liable to UK income tax on their UK income.

Spanish Residence

The first point to note is that the Spanish tax year is based on calendar years, unlike our tax year which runs from 6th April to 5th April. There are numerous rules regarding different levels of status in Spain:

- Individuals who spend more than 183 days in Spain during one calendar year must apply for a Spanish resident card, and be classed as permanent residents. These days do not have to be consecutive. You do not become a resident for tax purposes until the morning of the 184th day. However, as from the 2007 tax year the Spanish resident card (known as a 'residencia') has effectively been withdrawn. As such you would look to notify the local town hall within three months of your arrival.

- Temporary absences from Spain are ignored for the purpose of this rule unless it can be proved that the individual is habitually resident in another country for more than 183 days in a calendar year.

- If you arrive in Spain with the intention of living there indefinitely, the Spanish tax authorities (known as the 'Hacienda') will treat you as Spanish resident from the day after your arrival.

- If your spouse lives in Spain, you will be presumed to be a resident of Spain, provided you are not separated/divorced even though you may actually spend fewer than 183 days per year in Spain.

- If you live on a boat within 12 nautical miles of Spanish land, you are classed as a Spanish tax resident. A day within 12 nautical miles is a day spent in Spain for tax purposes.

It is clear that following the UK and Spanish domestic residence rules (above) an individual can be resident in both the UK and Spain. This is where it is important to identify how the double taxation agreement regulates matters.

How Does the UK/Spain Treaty Affect Matters?

The UK/Spain Double Tax Treaty has a 'tie-breaker' clause that comes into effect if an individual is classed as resident in the UK and Spain (under the domestic rules outlined above). This clause determines which country is to be given sole taxing rights, and prevents an individual being subject to UK and Spanish taxes on the same income.

The double tax agreement states that:

- If an individual is resident in both Spain and the UK, according to the domestic tax rules, he is to be deemed resident in the country in which he has a permanent home.

- If he has permanent homes in both Spain and the UK, he is deemed to be resident in the country that is classed as his centre of vital interests. This is a vague term, although it is generally regarded as the country with which an individual has the strongest ties and will therefore include both personal and financial connections.

- If it's still not possible to determine which country has the taxing rights, the country in which he has his habitual abode will be his country of residence.

- If he has an habitual abode in the UK and Spain, he will be resident in the country in which he is a national.

Example

Bob, a UK resident, owns a villa in Spain. If he occupies the villa for three months he will be a UK (not Spanish) resident, liable to UK income tax. If Bob rents out the villa, both the UK and Spanish tax authorities are likely to want a piece of the action. Although non-resident in Spain, Bob's rental income will have a Spanish source so Spanish tax will be payable. The UK tax authorities will be interested because Bob is UK resident, therefore subject to UK income tax on his worldwide income. In this case, the UK-Spain double tax treaty gives both countries the right to tax the income, so Bob will pay UK income tax and Spanish income tax (at the non-resident rate of 24.75% for 2012 on the gross income, with no deductions for expenses or interest costs). Bob must keep copies of his Spanish tax returns so he can offset the Spanish tax against his UK tax.

Assuming that Bob is a UK higher-rate taxpayer, and receives rental income of £10,000 and incurs costs of £2,000. The Spanish income tax liability would be £2,475 (£10,000 x 24.75%). UK tax would be £10,000 - £2,000 x 40% = £3,200.

Bob would then be entitled to deduct the Spanish income tax paid from the UK tax. The net effect is that Bob would actually pay £3,200 in income tax on the villa (£2,475 in Spain and £725 in the UK).

What Else Does the Double Tax Treaty Say?

The treaty has specific rules that will apply to certain types of income, irrespective of the domestic tax laws of the UK or Spain.

Under the domestic tax legislation of the UK and Spain it is easily possible for income to fall within the UK and Spanish tax systems. This is clearly unfair, and both the UK and Spain provide for a system of double tax relief where there is an element of double taxation.

However, in order to minimise this double tax the treaty has specifically stated in which country certain types of income will be taxed, when both countries may have a claim on the same income. The summarised rules are as follows:

Rental Income

The general rule is that this is taxed in the country where you are resident. Therefore once you become a resident in Spain, you will have to pay income tax on the rental income to the Spanish revenue authorities. However, the treaty also states that "income from immovable property... may be taxed in the Contracting State in which such property is situated".

In the case of a Spanish resident owning UK property, you would therefore still have to pay income tax on the rental income you derive from your UK property to UK Revenue and Customs.

The non-resident landlord scheme, which forces tenants and letting agents to pay over tax on behalf of overseas property owners, would then apply to collect UK tax. This means that you would pay tax in the UK as well as Spain, but would look to double tax relief to claim a deduction for the UK tax suffered. This would then prevent the rental income being taxed twice.

Dividends, Interest and Pension Income

The dividend and interest provisions give the primary right to tax dividends and interest to the country where the recipient is resident. Therefore a Spanish resident individual receiving dividend income or interest from a UK resident company or bank would pay income tax in Spain under the terms of the double taxation agreement.

The treaty would also allow the UK to tax the income if it wished (subject to some limitations). However, as we've seen under the UK tax rules, there would usually be no UK tax liability on UK-sourced dividends or bank interest for a non-UK resident.

Pensions, apart from Government Service Pensions, are specifically stated to be only taxable in the country of residence. This is provided by Article 18 of the UK-Spain double tax treaty which states:

"(1) Subject to the provisions of Article 19 pensions and other similar remuneration paid in consideration of past employment to a resident of a Contracting State and any annuity paid to such a resident shall be taxable only in that State."

Therefore a non-governmental pension paid from the UK to a Spanish resident would not be subject to UK income tax. If the pension was from the UK Government (for example, if you worked as a civil servant or a police officer etc) it would then, however, be taxed only in the UK (unless you were both a Spanish resident and a Spanish national, in which case it would again be taxable only in Spain).

Property Capital Gains

These are taxed in the country where the property is situated, as well as the country of residence. However most expats disposing of a UK property would be exempt from UK capital gains tax provided they satisfied the UK rules (for example, non-resident and not ordinarily resident for five complete tax years). In this case the tax liability would therefore primarily be a Spanish liability and this would be at a rate of 21%.

You will see that whilst the domestic concepts of residence for UK and Spain are important, the double tax treaty certainly simplifies matters, as it basically tells us which country's rules to use. When considering a move to any country you should consider whether a double tax treaty exists and how this will impact on the tax treatment of income and gains.

If you remain a UK resident you'll need to determine the impact of both UK and Spanish taxes.

Changes to UK and Spanish Capital Gains Tax

Anyone who owns a property in Spain may well be aware of the recent changes to the capital gains tax regime.

As from 1 January 2010 you would be subject to Spanish CGT at 19%. Residents will be taxed at 21% on gains above €6,000.

From 1 January 2012 these rates have changed. Non Spanish residents are subject to CGT at 21%, whereas residents are taxed at 21%, 25% or 27% depending on the size of the capital gain.

Spanish residents enjoy other advantages over non-residents:

- If you are over 65 years of age, and have lived in the property for three years or more, you will not be subject to capital gains tax when you sell.

- If the property is your principal residence and you have owned it for at least three years you can claim part or all of the tax back if you buy another principal residence within two years.

UK capital gains tax was recently changed for disposals taking place after 22nd June 2010. The flat 18% tax rate has been replaced by two rates: 18% for basic-rate taxpayers and 28% for higher-rate taxpayers.

How these Changes Will Affect You

If you own a Spanish property and are UK resident, will these changes have any impact on you? The short answer is yes.

As a UK resident you are usually taxed on your worldwide income and gains. Any gain will be reduced by the annual capital gains tax exemption (£10,600 for the 2012/13 tax year). If you're a higher-rate taxpayer and sell after 22nd June 2010 you'll pay UK CGT at 28%.

As well as UK CGT you'll be subject to Spanish CGT, as the property is in Spain. The UK-Spain double tax treaty states that:

"...Capital gains from the alienation of immovable property, as defined in paragraph (2) of Article 6, may be taxed in the Contracting State in which such property is situated..."

Therefore you will be taxed in the UK and Spain, although the treaty, as well as UK domestic tax law, allows the Spanish tax to be offset against your UK tax.

As the Spanish CGT rate is less than the UK rate if you are a higher-rate taxpayer this means that the UK tax will be partially offset by the Spanish tax charge. In practice, however, there are additional factors to consider because gains are calculated differently in each country. For example, in the UK the annual CGT exemption could reduce a gain by over £21,200 for a couple, resulting in even lower effective capital gains tax rates. Similarly in Spain there is something called the 'indexation coefficient' which can reduce the amount of tax payable.

If the gain is relatively small (for example, £80,000) the two annual CGT exemptions (for properties owned jointly) could significantly reduce the effective tax rate. For example, a gain of £80,000 would be reduced to £58,800. Tax at 28% would be £16,464, producing an effective tax rate of 21%.

14.7 CAPITAL GAINS TAX IN OTHER COUNTRIES

Most countries adopt similar provisions to those above, with the result that both the UK and overseas country would have taxing rights over capital gains. One of the few treaties that doesn't apply this rule is the one between the UK and Greece, which states:

"A resident of one of the territories who does not carry on a trade or business in the other territory through a permanent establishment situated therein shall be exempt in that other territory from any tax on gains from the sale, transfer or exchange of capital assets."

The effect of this would be that if you are a resident of Greece and own UK property you would not be subject to UK CGT when you sell the property. Of course, in most cases this will not be important because if you are a resident of Greece you'd be non-UK resident and possibly exempt from UK capital gains tax anyway.

The main use of the Greece treaty used to be to avoid the five-year absence rule for UK capital gains. However, as we've seen, this rule has now been amended so that it cannot be circumvented by using a double tax treaty.

If you are serious about avoiding both UK and overseas tax on the disposal of UK properties you need to satisfy the five-year rule to avoid UK capital gains tax and make sure that the overseas country in which you are resident will not itself tax the gain.

There are different ways that you can avoid paying taxes overseas. The overseas country may simply levy no taxes at all, or it may levy income tax but not capital gains tax, or it may apply a territorial basis and just tax local income and gains. There are lots of countries that could be used to avoid tax on any UK property investment gains including the Caribbean tax havens, Cyprus, the Isle of Man, Malta, and Monaco.

We've covered these in more detail in our guide, *The World's Best Tax Havens.*

If you are not disposing of land or property but disposing of shares in a company the treatment in the double tax treaty could vary a lot more.

The new UK-France treaty (in force from April 2010), for instance, states that:

"...Gains from the alienation of any property other than that referred to in paragraphs 1, 2, 3 and 4 (paragraphs 1,2,3 and 4 primarily relate to land, property and assets used in a permanent establishment) shall be taxable only in the Contracting State of which the alienator is a resident..."

"...The provisions of paragraph 5 shall not affect the right of a Contracting State to levy according to its law a tax chargeable in respect of gains from the alienation of any property on a person who is, and has been at any time during the previous six fiscal years, a resident of that Contracting State or on a person who is a resident of that Contracting State at any time during the fiscal year in which the property is alienated..."

220

So, if you are a French resident and have been a UK resident at any time in the previous six years and sold other UK assets (eg shares in a UK company), you could be taxed in the UK. As stated previously, the five-year residence exemption would apply anyway. You'd be subject to French taxes, though, on the basis that you were a French resident.

By contrast, the UK-Denmark treaty doesn't expressly cover the position of a disposal of shares and states:

"...Gains from the alienation of any property other than that referred to in paragraphs (1), (2), (3) and (4) of this Article, shall be taxable only in the Contracting State of which the alienator is a resident..."

This would allocate sole taxing rights over the shares disposal to Denmark. In both cases the overseas country of residence would obtain a right to tax the gain, the difference is that in the latter the treaty would only allow Denmark to tax the gain unless you went back to the UK without satisfying the five-year absence rule.

14.8   COUNTRIES WITHOUT A UK DOUBLE TAX TREATY

The UK has double tax treaties with lots of countries. These provide relief from double tax. The most common cases when a double tax treaty will apply are when interest or pensions are paid in one country to people living in another state.

The purpose of these treaties is not just to provide tax relief but also to allow the easy exchange of information between two countries. This will often be to verify that an individual is a tax resident overseas, and also to alert the overseas state to sources of income (for example, UK dividends).

It also makes sense to know which countries do *not* have a detailed treaty with the UK. In particular, if you're looking for enhanced privacy protection the lack of a double tax treaty can assist. As well as looking at double tax treaties though you should also look at whether there is a separate information exchange agreement between the UK and the relevant overseas country.

Both the G20 and OECD are looking to increase international tax cooperation and you'll therefore see many more information exchange treaties being signed over the next few years.

In terms of tax treaties, however, the following countries do not currently have a treaty with the UK:

Abu Dhabi	Equatorial	Northern Mariana
Afghanistan	Guinea	Islands
Albania	Eritrea	Palau
Algeria	French Polynesia	Panama
Andorra	Gabon	Paraguay
Angola	Gibraltar	Peru
Aruba	Guam	Puerto Rico
Bahamas	Guatemala	Rwanda
Bahrain	Guinea	St Lucia
Benin	Guinea-Bissau	St Vincent
Bermuda	Haiti	Samoa
Bhutan	Honduras	San Marino
Brazil	Iran	Sao Tome & Prin.
British Virgin Islands	Iraq	Senegal
Burkina Faso	Korea	Seychelles
Burundi	Laos	Somalia
Cambodia	Lebanon	Surinam
Cameroon	Liberia	Syria
Cape Verde	Libya	Tanzania
Central African Rep	Liechtenstein	Togo
Chad	Maldives	Tonga
Chile	Mali	United Arab
Colombia	Marshall Islands	Emirates
Comoros	Mauritania	Uruguay
Congo,	Micronesia	Vanuatu
Cook Islands	Monaco	US Virgin Islands
Costa Rica	Mozambique	
Cuba	Nauru	
Djibouti	Nepal	
Dominica	Neth. Antilles	
Dominican Republic	New Caledonia	
Ecuador	Nicaragua	
El Salvador	Niger	

As you can see there are quite a few and it's worth noting that many of these are tax havens or at the very least offer certain tax saving opportunities (for example, many have no capital gains tax).

14.9   HOW AN ESTATE TAX TREATY CAN BE USED

Although the above income tax treaties are very handy in terms of reducing taxes on income and gains they're completely useless if you're trying to assess your inheritance tax position. The reason for this is that the 'Taxes Covered' section of tax treaties does not cover inheritance tax.

The UK does have some inheritance tax treaties, however these are much fewer in number. There are around nine in total with France, Switzerland, Italy, India, South Africa, the US and Sweden. The technical name for these is 'Estate and Inheritance Tax Agreement' and they determine how each country will share out the tax collected from your estate.

Importance of Domicile

The key issue in terms of UK inheritance tax is domicile. Forget residence and even ordinary residence, inheritance tax looks at something much more substantive. As well as domicile, the location of assets is also important. As we've seen, the UK Revenue will tax:

- UK domiciliaries on their worldwide estate,
- Non-UK domiciliaries on their UK estate only

An estate tax treaty will be relevant where someone is subject to inheritance tax in more than one country. This could be a UK domiciliary with assets overseas. In this case the overseas assets would be within the scope of UK tax and also within the scope of overseas tax, as many countries have similar rules to the UK and tax assets within their jurisdiction.

There is also a much wider interpretation which arises because a person can remain UK domiciled despite not setting foot in the UK for ten years. As many overseas countries base inheritance tax on *residence*, you could easily have two countries trying to tax all of a deceased's worldwide assets: The UK on the basis of a UK domicile and the overseas country on the basis of residence.

The treaty will be very important in these cases as it lays out the tax rights of each country.

The Importance of Establishing Treaty Domicile

The UK estate tax treaties specifically provide for the UK domicile rules to apply but they also address the case where two countries are claiming the right to tax a person on his worldwide assets. Let's have a look at an extract from a treaty and see exactly what it states. In this case we'll look at the UK-Switzerland treaty:

Article 4

Fiscal domicile
(1) For the purposes of this Convention, a deceased person was domiciled: (a) in the United Kingdom if he was domiciled in the United Kingdom in accordance with the law of the United Kingdom or is treated as so domiciled for the purposes of a tax which is the subject of the Convention; (b) in Switzerland if he was domiciled or was resident in Switzerland in accordance with the law of Switzerland or if he was a Swiss national and Swiss civil law requires his succession to be ruled in Switzerland.

Note that the Convention defines the scope of fiscal domicile separately for the UK and for Switzerland. In the case of the UK it will also include the deemed domicile rules. These state that a person will be deemed to be UK domiciled for inheritance tax purposes if they are resident in the UK for 17 out of the previous 20 years and also for three years after they actually lose UK domicile status.

However, a deceased person will not be deemed to be domiciled in one of the states if that state imposes tax only by reference to property situated in that state. So a UK domiciliary owning property in Switzerland would not be classed as Swiss domiciled just because he owns property there.

(2) Where by reason of the provisions of paragraph (1) of this Article a deceased person was domiciled in both States, then, subject to the provisions of the attached Protocol, his status shall be determined as follows: (a) he shall be deemed to have been domiciled in the State in which he had a permanent home available to him; if he had a permanent home available to him in both States, he shall be deemed to have been domiciled in the State with which his personal and economic relations were closer (centre of vital interests); (b) if the State in which he had his centre of vital interests cannot be determined, or if he did not

have a permanent home available to him in either State, he shall be deemed to have been domiciled in the State in which he had an habitual abode; (c) if he had an habitual abode in both States or in neither of them, he shall be deemed to have been domiciled in the State of which he was a national; (d) if he was a national of both States or of neither of them, the competent authorities of the Contracting States shall settle the question by mutual agreement.

This is how the treaty determines which country will have primary taxing rights for inheritance tax purposes. These are exactly the same tests as many income tax treaties apply, in that it will be necessary to first look at the country of permanent residence, and if this does not determine domicile, the centre of vital interests would be determined. It is rarely necessary to look at other issues, but if necessary habitual abode and nationality could also be important factors.

Therefore if a UK domiciliary had property in the UK and Switzerland, but was a resident of Switzerland, the treaty would usually apply to give Switzerland taxing rights over the worldwide estate. If this individual also had assets located overseas this could lead to a significant tax saving given that Swiss inheritance tax is much lower than UK inheritance tax.

In this respect obtaining permanent residence in a treaty country can be highly beneficial for UK domiciliaries as it can eliminate the potential risk of a UK inheritance tax charge on your worldwide estate. Instead you'll only be taxed in the overseas country.

It makes sense, if you're planning to emigrate to a country with which the UK has an estate tax treaty, to establish treaty domicile there (a permanent home in the country concerned) to avoid the risk of double taxation.

The interpretation of double tax treaties is a complex area, and you should always take advice from an international tax specialist.

Chapter 15

Buying Property Abroad

15.1 INTRODUCTION

A lot of UK property investors are thinking about buying property abroad. Many are interested in the emerging markets of Eastern Europe (Latvia, Poland, Bulgaria and the like). Others stick to traditional favourites such as France, Italy and Spain.

There is a tendency amongst investors to get caught up in the excitement of owning an overseas property and neglect certain important financial issues, such as how any income and capital gains will be taxed.

The UK tax treatment will depend primarily on the tax status of the purchaser. Let's have a look at the UK tax implications for different types of purchaser, pooling together what we've learned in previous chapters.

15.2 UK RESIDENT/ORDINARILY RESIDENT AND DOMICILED

Any income and gains arising from the property will in the first instance be liable to UK taxes in full. The property will also be included within your estate for inheritance tax purposes.

Example

Jake is resident and domiciled in the UK. He decides to purchase a property in Latvia for letting during the summer months and for his own occupation during the winter. The rental income will be subject to UK income tax. Any gain/profit on a subsequent disposal will be liable to UK capital gains tax (less various reliefs). If he were to die whilst still owning the Latvian property, this would be taken into account when assessing the amount of inheritance tax he would pay.

15.3 NON-RESIDENT/ORDINARILY RESIDENT AND NON-UK DOMICILED

As you would expect, as a non-resident, any income and gains from the overseas property will not be liable to UK taxes. Similarly, the property would not be included within the individual's estate for inheritance tax purposes.

Example

Jacob, originally born in Portugal, has lived in Spain for 15 years and is regarded as non-UK resident and non-UK domiciled. His Spanish property would not be subject to UK taxes.

Note that for capital gains tax purposes, an individual must be non-resident for five complete tax years before being exempted from UK capital gains tax on assets held at the date of their emigration.

This provision was enacted in 1998 to prevent people with large potential gains in assets, becoming non-resident for a tax year, disposing of the asset and avoiding UK capital gains tax.

15.4 UK RESIDENT/ORDINARILY RESIDENT AND NON-UK DOMICILED

Individuals who are UK resident but non-UK domiciled have a number of advantages when it comes to UK taxes. Such individuals are typically foreign nationals (usually born overseas) who have come to live in the UK for a number of years.

The key aspect will be that for income tax and capital gains tax the remittance basis can apply. This means that any rental income from overseas property would be exempt from UK taxes provided the income is not remitted to the UK. In addition, on a future disposal no UK capital gains tax would be payable provided the sale proceeds are retained overseas.

As discussed in previous chapters, as from 6th April 2008 any non domiciliaries wanting to take advantage of this remittance basis will have to claim it (unless the overseas income or gains are less than £2,000). As well as losing certain UK allowances, if they've been UK resident for more than 7 of the last 10 tax years they will be subject to the annual £30,000 tax charge. This rises to £50,000 after 12 years of UK residence.

Therefore in practice a non UK domiciliary with an overseas property, paying income tax at the higher rate, may be looking to take advantage of the remittance basis where:

- They have been UK resident for 7 or less of the last 10 tax years; or

- They already have significant overseas unremitted income that makes paying the £30,000 or £50,000 charge tax efficient (e.g., over around £83,000 or £133,000 per tax year respectively).

- They are selling the overseas property and are realising a substantial capital gain to be retained overseas.

Again, from a UK tax perspective, there would be no UK inheritance tax impact. As a non-UK domiciliary, your estate would include only UK assets.

Example

Petra has lived in the UK for 5 years but has retained her overseas domicile. Petra has purchased a property in Monaco. She plans to rent this out for two years and then dispose of it for a (hopefully!) significant profit.

Provided Petra claims the remittance basis, retains the income overseas (for example, in an offshore bank account) and doesn't bring it into the UK, there will be no UK income tax charge. The same principle will apply to the sale proceeds. This will allow Petra to build up a tax-free amount that she could use to purchase further offshore properties.

Similarly, the property would not be classed as part of Petra's estate for inheritance tax purposes (being non-UK property of a non-UK domiciliary).

One thing to watch out for are the 'deemed domicile' rules. These apply for inheritance tax purposes only and state that individuals are deemed to have a UK domicile:

- If they have been UK resident for 17 out of the last 20 years, or

- They have lost their UK domicile in the last three years.

Example

In the above example, assume Petra has been living in the UK since 1970. For income tax purposes and capital gains tax purposes, Petra is of non-UK domicile. However, for inheritance tax purposes, she is deemed UK domicile as she has lived in the UK since 1970 and would therefore have been resident for more than 17 years.

Therefore for inheritance tax purposes, Petra would be subject to UK inheritance tax on her worldwide estate. This would mean that the property in Monaco could potentially be subject to UK inheritance tax.

In addition, as she has been UK resident for 12 or more of the past 14 years she would need to pay an annual £50,000 tax charge to take advantage of the remittance basis.

Non-UK domiciliaries can have a useful tax advantage when considering investing in overseas property. If they invest shortly after arrival they will have an 8 year window during which they can claim the remittance basis on overseas rental income and capital gains.

After this, provided they claim the remittance basis and reinvest proceeds offshore, they can limit their UK tax charge to £30,000 until they have been resident for 12 years. They can later bring the overseas taxed income back to the UK free of tax once all other untaxed overseas income has been remitted.

Where capital gains are expected to be significant (for example where more than one overseas property was sold in a tax year) this could result in a significant increase in the size and value of their investment portfolios as it enables them to reinvest in more overseas properties. This can give a useful boost to an offshore property portfolio.

15.5 USE OF AN OFFSHORE COMPANY/TRUST

A common misconception is that an offshore company or trust can be used in virtually all situations to avoid UK taxes. Unfortunately this is not true. For UK resident and domiciled individuals the UK tax authorities have a number of powerful anti-avoidance measures at their disposal.

This essentially allows the taxman to deem income to be subject to UK tax in a number of situations. It is therefore only in a number of limited situations that UK residents and domiciliaries can use offshore companies/trusts to avoid UK taxes.

As from April 2008, the Revenue will not be looking to levy a UK benefit-in-kind tax charge when a person buys an overseas property via a company, and then occupies that property. In practice, however, there are many other tax issues to be considered when buying an overseas property through a company.

Not least is the fact that using a company may well substantially increase the tax bill when the property is eventually sold.

Non-UK domiciliaries can, however, still make good use of offshore trusts to purchase overseas property provided the remittance basis applies. The trust would not be subject to UK inheritance tax as the assets of the trust would be overseas assets.

From a capital gains tax perspective, the trustees would not be liable to UK capital gains tax, as the trust would be non-resident. Provided the creator of the trust retains his non-UK domicile status, the UK anti-avoidance provisions attributing/deeming gains would not apply provided he is not a beneficiary. If he was a beneficiary then the remittance basis would apply in terms of capital payments from the trust.

Provided the overseas jurisdiction does not levy capital gains tax, there would also be no overseas tax charge (for example, in the Isle of Man).

Another useful opportunity for the non-UK domiciliary is to ensure that UK assets are owned by a non-resident company, of which the non-domiciliary is a 100% shareholder.

230

This would then ensure that the individual owns offshore assets (exempt from inheritance tax for non-UK domiciliaries) as opposed to UK assets (charged to UK inheritance tax).

15.6 USING MIXED RESIDENCE PARTNERSHIPS TO AVOID CGT

Another option that could be considered is using a partnership.

There are occasions where a UK resident (individual A) is looking to invest in overseas property but may also have a *non-resident* friend, relative or business partner (individual B) who will be undertaking the investment with them. The question is how should they structure the property purchases?

They could keep the purchases in the name of the non-resident. As a non-resident and not ordinarily resident individual, B would be outside the scope of UK capital gains tax. A, as a UK resident individual, would be subject to CGT on any gains arising. The problem with this arrangement is that it is unlikely to be commercially acceptable to A, who would want to have some entitlement to the assets.

A further problem is that, for tax purposes, HMRC would look to the *beneficial* ownership of the property as opposed to the strict legal ownership. Therefore even if title was solely in B's name, if A would be entitled to a share of any rental income and proceeds of disposal there is a risk that HMRC could assess a share of the gain on A in any case, and therefore UK capital gains tax would be charged.

This is where a partnership may be beneficial. If they were to use a partnership structure the general rule is that each partner would be assessed on their share of the partnership's profits and gains. In this case, however, the partnership would be a mixed residence partnership (as B would be non-resident, and A would be UK resident). This complicates matters and special rules relating to mixed residence partnerships would need to be considered.

In this case it would be necessary to look at the control and management of the partnership (in a similar way that HMRC would look to see if an offshore company was controlled from the UK). If the control and management of a partnership carrying on a trade or business is situated outside the UK the business is deemed to be carried on by individuals not resident in the UK. For CGT purposes, a partner in such a partnership is treated as if he were not resident in the UK (but only in relation to disposals of that partnership's assets).

Therefore, provided they could show the management and control of the partnership was overseas, and that the partnership was engaged in a business, for capital gains tax purposes, both A and B should be exempt from UK capital gains tax. Note that in terms of any rental profit, A would still be within the scope of UK income tax.

Establishing an overseas residence for the partnership would be a complex area. However, as when looking at the residence of an overseas company, HMRC would tend to look at the place of the highest level of management rather than day-to-day management.

They would usually look at factors such as the location of partners' meetings, the seniority of the partners in age and experience and where major transactions were undertaken.

A and B could also consider having equal capital sharing ratios (to split capital equally) but giving the non-resident partner a higher profit sharing ratio to increase his interest in the partnership and possibly increase the likelihood of establishing the partnership offshore. Any planning involving using an offshore partnership would need to be carefully considered with your professional adviser.

15.7   WHAT ABOUT OVERSEAS TAX IMPLICATIONS?

Of course the downside to all of the above is that we have only looked at the UK tax implications. Many countries retain the right to tax:

- Residents, and
- Assets of non-residents located within their jurisdiction.

Therefore, anyone considering purchasing a property overseas should take advice from a relevant tax professional as to how any income or gain will be taxed locally.

In the case of Spain, for example, individuals are taxed at a standard 21% on any gains arising on a disposal and 24.75% on the gross rental income.

In addition, the 'standard' double tax treaty that most countries choose to adopt would treat the income/gain as being sourced from the country in which the property is located and therefore subject to the overseas tax regime. It would therefore only be if a property was purchased in a 'tax haven' that liability could be avoided. Such tax havens include Andorra, Monaco, and the Cayman Islands.

15.8   DOUBLE TAX RELIEF (DTR)

If you are subject to tax both in the UK and overseas, there are provisions designed to ensure that you don't pay tax twice. As mentioned earlier this is known as double tax relief (DTR) and you can claim DTR against your UK tax charge.

DTR is given as the lower of:

- The UK tax on the overseas income
- The overseas tax

Therefore, if the overseas tax was charged at 50%, with UK tax being 40%, you would obtain DTR at 40%. Similarly, if the overseas tax was charged at 20% and UK tax 40%, you would only obtain DTR at 20%. The net effect of this is that you will be left paying the highest tax charge.

Example

Richard, a UK resident individual has the following income in the 2012/13 tax year:

UK salary	*£50,000*
UK dividends (gross)	*£2,000*
Overseas rental income	*£3,000*
(50% overseas tax paid)	

His tax calculation would be:

Salary from UK employment	*£50,000*
Overseas income	*£3,000*
UK dividends	*£2,000*
Less personal allowance	*-£8,105*
Taxable income	*£46,895*

The income tax levied on this taxable income would be reduced by double tax relief.

As the overseas income will be subject to tax at the higher rate (as the taxable income exceeds the UK higher rate tax band), we can calculate that the double tax relief will be the lower of

- *The UK tax on overseas income (40% x £3,000) = £1,200*
- *The overseas tax (50% x £3,000) = £1,500*

Therefore total double tax relief in this case would be £1,200 (lowest of the two figures) and this would be given as a credit against Richard's tax liability.

15.9 SUMMARY

The tax implications of purchasing a property overseas are certainly not straightforward and you should always consider carefully the UK and (just as importantly) the overseas tax implications.

By way of a summary, I would suggest that the following points be borne in mind when purchasing a property overseas:

- Assess your residence/domicile position to ascertain your liability to UK taxes.

- Obtain overseas tax advice to determine what rate of taxes (if any) exist overseas.

- Retain all receipts (for example, conveyancing fees, valuations, agency fees) – these can be offset when calculating any gain charged to UK capital gains tax.

- Keep full information/documentation of any tax suffered on overseas income/gains – this will be required to substantiate a DTR claim, should HMRC ask questions after you submit your tax return.

- Think about the most effective structure for the purchase, whether by you individually or via a company or trust.

- If you are a non-UK domiciliary, watch out for the deemed domicile rules and consider getting advice from a professional about establishing an offshore trust. It's best to do this sooner rather than later. It is the status of the trust creator at the date the trust is established that is crucial for inheritance tax purposes (and is for capital gains tax and income tax purposes after 6th April 2007). If you later became a UK domiciliary, the trust assets would still be exempt from UK inheritance tax.

Appendix I: UK-Spain Double Tax Treaty

ARTICLE 13 UK SPAIN DOUBLE TAX TREATY

(1) Capital gains from the alienation of immovable property, as defined in paragraph (2) of Article 6, may be taxed in the Contracting State in which such property is situated.

(2) Capital gains from the alienation of movable property forming part of the business property of a permanent establishment which an enterprise of a Contracting State has in the other Contracting State or of movable property pertaining to a fixed base available to a resident of a Contracting State in the other Contracting State for the purpose of performing professional services, including such gains from the alienation of such a permanent establishment (alone or together with the whole enterprise) or of such a fixed base, may be taxed in the other State.

(3) Notwithstanding the provisions of paragraph (2) of this Article, capital gains derived by a resident of a Contracting State from the alienation of ships and aircraft operated in international traffic and movable property pertaining to the operation of such ships and aircraft shall be taxable only in that Contracting State.

(4) Capital gains from the alienation of any property other than those mentioned in paragraphs (1), (2) and (3) of this Article shall be taxable only in the Contracting State of which the alienator is a resident.

ARTICLE 24(4)

Income and capital gains owned by a resident of a Contracting State which may be taxed in the other Contracting State in accordance with this Convention shall be deemed to arise from sources in that other Contracting State.

Appendix II: UK Treatment of Overseas Entities

ANGUILLA Partnership	Transparent
ARGENTINA Sociedad de responsibilidad limitada	Opaque
AUSTRIA KG Kommanditgesellschaft	Transparent
KEG Kommand Erwerbsgesellschaft	Transparent
GmbH & Co KG	Transparent
GmbH Gesellschaft mit Beschrankter Haftung	Opaque
AG Aktiengesellschaft	Opaque
BELGIUM SPRL Societe de privee a responsabilite	Opaque
SNC Societe en nom collectif	Transparent
SA Societe Anonyme	Opaque
NV Naamloze Vennootschap	Opaque
SCA Societe en commanditaire par actions	Opaque
CVA Commanditaire venootschap op aandelen	Opaque
BRAZIL Srl Sociedad por quotas de responabilidade	Opaque
CANADA Partnership and limited partnership	Transparent
CAYMAN ISLANDS Limited partnership	Transparent
CHILE SRL Sociedad de responsibilidad limitada	Transparent
CHINA WFOE Wholly Foreign Owned Entity	Opaque
CZECH REPUBLIC as Akciova spolecnost	Opaque
SRO Spolecnost s rucenim omezenym	Opaque
EUROPEAN UNION SE Societas Europeas	Opaque
FINLAND Ky Kommandiittiyhtio	Transparent
Oy Osakeyhtio	Opaque
Ab Aktiebolag	Opaque
FRANCE GIE Groupement d'Interet economique	Transparent
SNC Societe en nom collectif	Transparent
SCI Societe civile immobiliere	Opaque
SCS Societe en commandite simple	Transparent
SP Societe en participation	Transparent
SARL Societe a responsabilite limitee	Opaque
FCPR Fonds Commun de Placement a risques	Transparent
SAS Societe par Actions Simplifiee	Opaque
SA Societe Anonyme	Opaque
GFA Groupement Foncier d'Agricole	Opaque
SC Societe Civile	Opaque
GERMANY Stille Gesellschaft	Opaque
KG Kommandit Gesellschaft	Transparent
OHG Offene Handelsgesellschaft	Transparent
GmbH & Co. KG	Transparent

AG Aktiengesellschaft	Opaque
GUERNSEY LP Limited Partnership	Transparent
PCC Protected Cell Company	Opaque
HUNGARY Kft Korlatolt felelossegu tarsasag	Opaque
Rt. Reszvenytarsasag	Opaque
ICELAND Hlutafelag	Opaque
IRELAND Limited Partnership	Transparent
Irish Investment Limited Partnership	Transparent
CCF Common Contractual Fund	Transparent
ITALY SpA Societa per Azioni	Opaque
JAPAN Goshi-Kaisha	Transparent
Gomei Kaisha	Transparent
TK Tokumei Kumiai	Transparent
Kabushikikaisha	Opaque
Yugen-kaisha	Opaque
JERSEY LLP Limited Liability Partnership	Opaque
KAZAKHSTAN LLC Limited Liability Company	Opaque
LIECHTENSTEIN Anstalt	Opaque
FCP Fonds commun de placement	Transparent
SA Societe anonyme	Opaque
SARL Societe a responsabilite limitee	Opaque
SJCAV Societe d'investment a capitale variable	Opaque
NETHERLANDS VOF Vennootschap Onder Firma	Transparent
CV Commanditaire Vennootschap	Transparent
NV Naamloze Vennootschap	Opaque
Maatschap	Transparent
Stichting	Transparent
Co-op Cooperatie	Transparent
NEW CALEDONIA SNC Societe en nom collectif	Transparent
NORWAY AS Alkjeselskap	Opaque
KS Kommandittselkap	Transparent
SA Sociedade Anonima	Opaque
RUSSIA Joint Venture under "Decree No.49"	Opaque
LLC Limited Liability Company	Opaque
SPAIN SC Sociedad Civila	Opaque
SA Sociedad Anonima	Opaque
Srl Sociedad de Responsabilidad Limitada	Opaque
SWEDEN AB Aktiebolag	Opaque
KB Kommanditbolag	Transparent
SWITZERLAND SS Societe Simple	Transparent
GmbH Gesellschaft mit beschrankter Haftung	Opaque
TURKEY AP Attorney Partnership	Transparent
AS Anonim Sirket	Opaque

Ltd/S Limited Sirket	Opaque
USA Limited	Transparent
LLC Limited Liability Company	Opaque
LLP Limited Liability Partnership	Transparent
MBT Massachusetts Business Trust	Transparent
S. Corp S. Corporation	Opaque

Lightning Source UK Ltd.
Milton Keynes UK
UKOW030904210512

192975UK00001B/6/P